SHAH JAHAN

SHAH JAHAN

BY

H. M. ELLIOT

GYAN

Published by

GYAN

Gyan Publishing House
5, Ansari Road
Daryaganj, New Delhi-110002
Phone: 011-47034999, 9811692060
E-mail: books@gyanbooks.com

Distribution Network
gyanbooks.com
India, USA, Canada, UK, Australia

ISBN: 978-93-6433-903-2 (HB)
First Published, 1875

2nd Impression 2024

Printed at: Gyan Press, Delhi.

SHAH JAHAN

AUTHOR: H. M. ELLIOT

SHAH JAHAN

CONTENTS

PADSHAH-NAMA

OF

MUHAMMAD AMIN KAZWINI

(The author of this work in his preface gives it the title of *Padshah-nama,* but, like several other histories of the reign of Shah Jahan, it is often called *Shah-Jahan-nama,* and sometimes more specifically *Tarikh-i Shah-Jahani Dah-sala*. The full name of the author is Muhammad Amin bin Abu-l Hasan Kazwini, but he is familiarly known as Aminai Kazwini, Aminai Munshi, or Mirza Amina. He was the first who received orders to write a history of the reign of Shah Jahan. The orders were given, as he tells us, in the eighth year of Shah Jahan, and he completed this work, comprising the history of the first ten years of the reign, and dedicated it to Shah Jahan in the twentieth year of that Emperor's reign.

The Author in his preface says that he has divided his work into an Introduction, containing an account of the Emperor's life from his birth to his accession; a Discourse (*makala*), comprising the history of the first ten years of his reign; and an Appendix, containing notices of holy and learned men, physicians and poets. He also mentions his intention of writing a second volume, bringing down the history to the twentieth year of Shah Jahan's reign. But he does not appear to have carried out his design, having probably been prevented by his appointment to a busy office, for Muhammad Salih, in a short biography of the author, says that he was transferred to the Intelligence Department.

This history of Aminai Kazwini has been the model upon which most of the histories of Shah Jahan have been formed. 'Abdu-l Hamid, the author of the *Badshah-nama,* follows its arrangement, and although he makes no acknowledgment of the fact, his work comprises the same matter, and differs from it only in style.

Sir H. M. Elliot's MS. is a small folio of 297 pages of twenty-one lines each. It is fairly written, but all the rubrics are omitted. There is a copy in the Library of the Royal Asiatic Society, and three copies in the British Museum.)[1]

[1](*This article has been taken almost exclusively from Morley's Catalogue of the MSS. of the Royal Asiatic Society.*).

BADSHAH-NAMA
OF
'ABDU-L HAMID LAHORI

(This is a history of the first twenty years of the reign of Shah Jahan, composed by 'Abdul Hamid Lahori. Little is known of the author, but Muhammad Salih, in his *'Amal-i Salih* informs us that 'Abdu-l Hamid was celebrated for the beauty of his style, and that he died in 1065 A.H. (1654 A.D.). 'Abdu-l Hamid himself says in his preface, that the Emperor desired to find an author who could write the memoirs of his reign in the style of Abu-l Fazl's *Akbar-nama;* and that he, 'Abdu-l Hamid, had studied and greatly admired Abu-l Fazl's style. He was recommended to the Emperor for the work, and was called from Patna, where he was living in retirement, to undertake the composition. His patron was the excellent minister 'Allami Sa'dulla Khan.

The contents of the work are: A Preface, in which the author dedicates his work to Shah Jahan. A description of the Emperor's horoscope. A concise account of his ancestors, commencing with Timur. A brief review of the proceedings of Shah Jahan before his accession to the throne. A detailed history of the first twenty years of the reign divided into two cycles of ten years each. The work comprises, also, an enumeration of the princes of the blood royal; of the nobles of the Court, arranged according to their respective ranks, from those commanding 9000 to those of 500 horse; and an account of the *shaikhs,* learned men, physicians and poets who flourished during the period embraced by the history.

The *Badshah-nama* is the great authority for the reign of Shah-Jahan. Muhammad Salih, a younger and rival writer, speaks of the author in the highest term, and "Khafi Khan, the author of the *Muntakhabu-l Lubab,* has based his history of the first twenty years of Shah Jahan's reign almost entirely on this work. The greatest objection to the work is the author's style, which is of that adulterated kind introduced into India apparently by the brothers Abu-l Fazl and Faizi."[2] 'Abdu-l Hamid was, as he himself states, a professed admirer and imitator of Abu-l Fazl's style; and when he is dealing with a subject demanding his eloquence, his style is as verbose, turgid and fulsome as that of his master. Happily, however, he is not always in a magniloquent vein, but narrates simple facts in simple language, blurred only by occasional outbreaks of his laboured rhetoric.

The work is most voluminous, and forms two bulky volumes of the Bibliotheca Indica, containing 1662 pages. It enters into most minute details of all the transactions in which the Emperor was engaged, the pensions and dignities conferred upon the various members of the royal family, the titles granted to the nobles, their changes of office, the augmentations of their *mansabs*, and it gives lists of all the various presents given and received on public occasions, such as the vernal equinox, the royal birthday, the royal accession, etc. Thus the work contains a great amount of matter of no interest to any one but the nobles and courtiers of the time. But it would not be fair to say that it is filled with these trifles; there is far too much of them: but still there is a solid substratum of historical matter, from which the history of this reign has been drawn by later writers.

MSS. of the *Badshah-nama* are common, and some fine copies are extant. Morley describes one belonging to the Royal Asiatic Society as "a most excellent specimen of the Oriental art of caligraphy," and Col. Lees says: "The copy of the second part of the *Badshah-*

[2] *Col. Lees, Jour. R.A. vol. iii. N.S.*

nama which has been used for this edition (Bibliotheca Indica) is the finest MS. I have ever seen. It is written by Muhammad Salih Kambu, the author of the *'Amal-i Salih,* and bears on the margin the autograph of the Emperor Shah Jahan." The following Extracts have all been selected and translated by the Editor from the printed text.)[3]

EXTRACTS

The Emperor Jahangir[4] died on the 28th Safar A.H. 1037 (28th October, 1627), at the age of fifty-eight years and one month, solar reckoning. Prince Shahriyar, from his want of capacity and intelligence, had got the nickname of *Na-shudani,* "Good-for-nothing" and was commonly known by that appellation. He now cast aside all honour and shame, and before Shah Jahan had started (from the Dakhin), he repudiated his allegiance, and went off in hot haste to Lahore to advance his own interests. Nur Mahal, who had been the cause of much strife and contention, now clung to the vain idea of retaining the reins of government in her grasp, as she had held them during the reign of the late Emperor. She wrote to Na-shudani, advising him to collect as many men as he could, and hasten to her.

Yaminu-d daula Asaf Khan and Iradat Khan, who always acted together determined that, as Shah Jahan was far way from Agra, it was necessary to take some steps to prevent disturbances in the city, and to get possession of the princes Muhammad Dara Shukoh, Muhammad Shah Shuja', and Muhammad Aurangzeb,

[3] *This article has been compiled by the Editor from 'Abdu-l Hamid's preface, Sir H. M. Elliot's notes, Morley's notice in the Catalogue of the Royal Asiatic Society, and Col. Lees' article in the Journal of the Royal Asiatic Society, vol. iii., N.S.*

[4] *His title after death was "Jannat-makani."*

who were in the female apartments with Nur Mahal. They therefore resolved that for some few days they would raise to the throne Bulaki, the son of Khusru, who, by Nur Mahal's contrivance, had been placed with Na-shudani, but who had been put under the charge of Iradat Khan by Jahangir when Na-shudani returned to Lahore from Kashmir.

. . . So they placed Bulaki on horseback, and, with a party of men in whom they had full confidence, they commenced their march, taking care to keep one day ahead of Nur-Mahal . . . . As the young princes were not safe with Nur Mahal, they removed her from the royal palace, and took the young princes under their own charge; but when Bulaki had been raised to the throne. they were placed in charge of Sadik Khan.

ACCESSION OF SHAH JAHAN

Shah Jahan ascended the throne at Agra on the 18th Jumada-s sani, 1037 A.H. (6th Feb. 1628), with the title of Abu-l Muzaffar Shahabu-d din Muhammad Sahib Kiran-i sani.

REBELLION OF JAJHAR SINCH

Jajhar Singh was son of Raja Nar Singh Deo Bundela, who rose into notice by killing Shaikh Abu-l Fazl, the celebrated author of the *Akbar-nama,* when Jahangir was heir apparent . . . In odedience to orders from the Emperor Akbar, the Shaikh was hastening to Court from the Dakhin with a small escort. Jahangir was jealous of the Shaikh's devotion to his father, and was apprehensive that his arrival would interefere with his own plans. . . . So he incited Nar Singh Deo to kill him as he passed through his territory. This evil-minded man, from lust of gold, placed a large force of horse and foot in ambush, and fell upon the Shiakh. The followers of the Shaikh advised him to fly and escape, but he refused, and fell in the year 1011 A.H.

(1602 A.D.). After the accession of Jahangir to the throne, Nar Singh Deo rose into favour and distinction through this wicked deed. But his evil nature was unable to bear his prosperity, and towards the end of the reign of Jahangir he became disaffected, and oppressed all the *zamindars* in his neighbourhood . . . He died three or four months before Jahangir, and was succeeded by his son Jajhar Singh. The wealth and property which Nar Singh Deo had amassed without labour and without trouble unsettled the mind of his worthless successor Jajhar, and at the accession of Shah Jahan, . . . he left the capital Agra, and proceeded to Undcha, his stronghold, where he set about raising forces, strengthening the forts, providing munitions of war and closing the roads. A force was accordingly sent against him, under the command of Mahabat Khan Khan-khanan. (*The Imperial forces converged upon Undcha, and*) Jajhar Singh, having no hope of escape, waited upon Khan-khanan and made his submission. Just at this time intelligence arrived that 'Abdu-lla Khan had taken the fortress of Irich,[5] which had been in the possession of Jajhar Singh.

SECOND YEAR OF THE REIGN, 1038 A.H. (20th DEC. 1628, A.D.)

The anniversary of the accession was on the 1st of Jumada-s sani. After the death of Jahangir, and before the accession of Shah Jahan, Khan-jahan Lodi entered upon a dangerous and disloyal course. . . . He formed an alliance with Nizamu-l Mulk, and gave up to him the Balaghat in the Dakhin,[6] the revenue of which amounted to fifty-five *krors* of *dams*. But Sipahdar Khan, who held Ahmadnagar, bravely and loyally refused to surrender that city. Khan-Jahan summoned to his presence all the Imperial servants who were

[5] *65 miles S.E. of Gwalior.*

[6] *Khafi Khan says the temptation was six lacs of pagodas.—"Muntakhabu-l Lubab."*

in those parts. He left a small force at Burhanpur under the command of Sikandar Dotani, who was related to him, while he himself marched with a large force to Mandu, with the intention of taking possession of Malwa, which province was then under the government of Mir 'Abdu-r Razzak, who had received the title of Muzaffar Khan. Shah Jahan proceeded from Ahmadbad by way of Ajmir to Agra, and there ascended the throne . . . The news of this event awakened Khan-Jahan and brought him to a sense of his folly and wickedness. Raja Gaj Singh, Raja Jai Singh, and other distinguished Rajputs who had accompanied him to Mandu, parted from him when they heard of Shah Jahan having arrived at Ajmir. Thereupon Khan-Jahan wrote a letter of contrition and obedience, in the hope of obtaining forgiveness.

A royal *farman* was sent in answer, informing him that he was confirmed in the governorship of the Dakhin, and directing him to return at once to Burhanpur. He then retired from Malwa to Burhanpur and engaged in the duties of his office. But when it was reported to the Emperor that the country of Balaghat, which Khan-Jahan had given to Nizamu-l Mulk, still remained in his possession, and had not been recovered, the Emperor appointed Mahabat Khan to the governorship of the Dakhin. Khan-Jahan then returned to Court. The Emperor paid little heed to the reports and observations about his improper conduct, and for eight months passed no rebuke upon him. He still continued moody and discontented and ready to listen to the incitements and suggestions of mischievous men. . . . One night Lashkari, son of Mukhlis Khan, in a malicious, mischief-making spirit, told the son of Khan-Jahan that he and his father were to be made prisoners on the following day or the next. . . . The son told his father, whose apprehensions were instantly aroused by this malicious report, and he kept close to his quarters with two thousand Afghan followers. His Majesty asked Yaminu-d daula Asaf Khan the reason why Khan-Jahan did not attend the *darbar*, and after inquiry had been made, it was ascertained that he had fears and suspicions, and he begged for a letter under the Emperor's signature, forgiving him all his offences, and relieving him from all his fears. . . . The Emperor graciously acceded to his request, and sent him a kind letter under his own hand. He then came to Court and paid his respects. But Fortune was aggrieved with him, and so his perverse temper prevented him from appreciating the Emperor's kindness.

On the night of Safar 26, the men of Yaminu-d daula brought in the intelligence that Khan-Jahan mediated flight, and he sent to inform the Emperor. . . . After the first watch of the night, Khan-Jahan, with his nephew Bahadur and other relations and adherents, began his flight. As soon as the Emperor was informed of it, he sent Khwaja Abu-l Hasan and . . . in pursuit of the fugitive. Unmindful of the smallness of their own force and the numbers of the Afghans, they followed them and overtook them in the vicinity of Dholpur.[7] The fugitives saw their road of escape was closed; for the waters of the Chambal were before them and the fire of the avenging sword behind. So they posted themselves in the rugged and difficult ground on the bank of the river, and, fearing to perish in the waters, they resolved upon battle. . . (*After many were killed and wounded*), Khan-Jahan, with his two sons and several followers, resolved to hazard the passage of the Chambal, although the water was running high. He and his followers, wounded and unwounded, in great peril and with great exertion, succeeded in crossing over, thus escaping from the fire of battle and the waters of the stream. Many horses and much baggage fell into the hands of the royal forces. .

[7] Dholpur is about thirty-five miles from Agra near the left bank of the Chambal.

A party gathered to follow up the fugitives, but on reaching the bank of the river, it was found that it could not be crossed without boats, and an endeavour was made to collect some. Khwaja Abu-l Hasan came up when one *pahar* of the day remained, and after consultation it was resolved to stay there for the night, and rest the horses which had made a long and fatigued march. Boats were collected, and the whole force passed over before noon next day, and recommenced the chase. But the fugitives pressed forward with all haste, and threw themselves into the jungles of Jajhar Singh Bundela.

When the traitor (Khan-Jahan) entered the territory of Jajhar Singh Bundela, that chieftain was absent in the Dakhin; but his eldest son Bikramajit was at home, and sent the rebel out of the territory by unfrequented roads. If Birkramajit had not thus favoured his escape, he would have been either taken prisoner or killed. He proceeded to Gondwana, and after staying there some time in disappointment and obscurity, he proceeded by way of Birar to the country of Burhan Nizamu-l Mulk.

THIRD YEAR OF THE REIGN, 1039 A.H. (1629 A.D.)

. On the 21st Ramazan Khwaja Abu-l Hasan and . . . . altogether about 8000 horse, were sent to effect the conquest of Nasik and Trimbak,[8] and Sangamnir. It was settled that the Khwaja was to stay at some suitable position near the fort of Alang[9] during the rainy season until he was joined by Sher Khan from the province of Gujarat with his provincial levies. After the end of the rains he was to march by way of Baglana, and, taking with him some of the *zamindars* of the coun-

[8] *This name is here written, "Tirbang" but afterwards "Tirambak" or "Trimbak." The real name is Tirambak or Trimbak. It is a little west of Nasik.*

[9] *The text here has "Lalang" but afterwards "Alang".*

try, make his way to Nasik. The Khwaja marched from Burhanpur, and in eight days reached the village of Dholiya[10] near the fort of Alang, and there halted until the rains should cease . . . Sher Khan, Subadar of Gujarat, joined with 26,000 men, and the Khwaja sent him to attack the fort of Batora, in the vicinity of Chandor, near Nasik and Trimbak. Sher Khan ravaged the country, and returned with great spoil.

MURDER OF JADU RAI

Jadu Rai, with his sons, grandsons, and other relations held altogether from the Imperial Government *mansabs* amounting to 24,000 (personal) and 15,000 horse. He also had sundry *jagirs* in the Dakhin as *tankhwah,* so that he lived in wealth and comfort. But he was fickle and unfaithful, and went with his sons and relations to join the Nizam. But the Nizam well knew his perfidy, and resolved to put him in confinement. For this purpose the Nizam arranged with some of his servants to seize Jadu Rai, and he summoned him to his presence. Accordingly Jadu attended the Court with his family. The armed men who were in concealment suddenly attacked them, and killed him, his two sons Ujla and Raghu. and his grandson Baswant. His brother Jagdeo Rai, with Bahadur-ji his son, his wife and the other who escaped, fled from Daulatabad to Sindghar, near Jalnapur,[11] in their native country.

CAMPAIGN AGAINST NIZAM SHAH AND KHAN-JAHAN

(Text, vol. i. p. 316). 7th Rabi'u-l awwal. When the rains were over, 'Azam Khan and the great nobles who were with him left Dewalganw[12] where they had rested

[10] *About half way between Burhanpur and Nasik.*
[11] *Or Jalna, east of Aurangabad.*
[12] *About* 60 *miles S. of Burhanpur.*

during the rainy season, and marched against the rebel Afghans. .

At the conclusion of the rains, Khwaja Abu-l Hasan also, according to orders, marched from the vicinity of the fort of Alang by way of Baglana towards Nasik and Trimbak. When he reached Baglana, the *zamindar* of that country, by name Bahar-ji, met him with four hundred horse. . . The Khwaja entered the enemy's country by way of the ghat of Jarahi. He found that the revenue officers and *raiyats* had left their villages, and had retired into the jungles and hills. So the country was desolate, corn was dear, and the soldiers of the royal army were in want of necessaries. The Khwaja then sent detached forces into the hills, and also into the inhabited country, and they returned from each raid with abundance of corn and other necessaries, having killed or taking prisoners many of the enemy. The Be-Nizam[13] now appointed Mahaldar Khan with a party of horse and foot to vex the royal army at night with rockets. He was also directed to attack the parties sent out to gather fuel and fodder, and to carry off their camels and bullocks whenever he could get a chance. Shah-nawaz Khan was sent against these assailants, and he, making a forced march of twenty *kos,* attacked them and put them to flight, and returned with great plunder. The Khwaja next sent Khan-zaman to attack the enemy's camp at Sangamnir. This force made forced marches, and reached the camp of the enemy, who dispersed and fled to the fort of Chandor. .

At the close of the rains, the royal army left its quarters in Dewalganw, and marched forth against the Nizam-Shahis and the Afghans. On hearing of this, Mukarrab Khan and the other rebels left Jalnapur, where

[13] *"No ruler". This is the nickname which the author invariably uses in referring to Nizam Shah.*

they had passed the rainy season, and retreated towards Pathri.[14] 'Azam Khan, being informed of their retreat, followed them march by march. When he reached the village of Rambhuri, on the Ban-ganga river, he learnt that the Nizam-Shahis had ascended the Balaghat at Dharur,[15] and had taken refuge in the fort of that place, while Khan-Jahan had not yet left his quarters at Bir. Khan-Jahan, having been informed of the movement of the Imperial army, called in a detachment which he had sent to collect the revenues in the dependencies of Bir, and awaited the arrival of reinforcements from Mukarrab Khan, who was at Dharur. 'Azam Khan conceived the design of attacking the forces of the rebel Khan before the reinforcements could reach him; so he marched from Rambhuri to Mahganw. Here he received a message from Saf-shikan Khan Razwi, commandant of the fort of Bir, informing him that Khan-Jahan was at Rajauri, twenty-four *kos* from Machhli-ganw, employed in dividing the spoil which his predatory followers had obtained by plundering the merchants at Kehun and Kiorai. Several detachments which had been sent out to make collections had rejoined him, and as he had heard of the arrival of the Imperial army at Pathri, he had made up his mind to move off as soon as it came nearer to Bir.

'Azam Khan left a detachment in charge of his camp at Machhliganw to follow him quietly while he marched off after night-fall to attack the rebels. Four *gharis* of night remained when he reached Pipalnir, six *kos* from Bir, when he directed Saf-shikan Khan to make a demonstration with his force on Khan-Jahan's flank, so that he might think this small force to be the whole of

[14] *Between the Purna and Godavari rivers, about thirty miles from their junction.*

[15] *Bir and Dharur both lie on the road east of Ahmadnagar.*

the royal army, and refrain from moving away. Saf-shikan Khan accordingly drew out his force upon a ridge about a *kos* in front of the rebel army, which had taken post at the foot of the hills about four *kos* from Bir. 'Aziz, son of Khan-Jahan, advanced to attack Saf-shikan with a body of his father's troops, and at this juncture 'Azam Khan came up with the main body of the royal army, and 'Aziz, was compelled to fall back in disorder to his father, whom he informed that the force which had first shown itself was Saf-shikan Khan's division, and that the whole of the royal army was coming up with all possible haste.

Khan-Jahan, when he found that his retreat was cut off, determined to fight it out. . . But the royal troops forced their way to the top of the hill. Khan-Jahan sent away the elephant litter with his women to Siu-ganw,[16] and then rallied his troops for a struggle. He sent his nephew Bahadur, in whose courage and daring he had great confidence, against Bahadur Khan and some others of the royal army, who, being few in number, were very hard pressed. They dismounted, and, resolving to sell their lives dearly, they kept up a desperate struggle, and slew many of the enemy. Bahadur Khan received two wounds from arrows, one in his face, the other in his side, and several of his comrades were slain.[17] Narhar Das also and many Rajputs fell. Sipahdar Khan and others, who had mounted the hill on the right, seeing the state of the battle, took shelter behind a stone wall. and kept up a discharge of arrows. Raja Bihar Singh Bundela now came up from the right wing to support Bahadur Khan. He joined valiantly in the struggle and

[16] *About 40 miles N.E. of Ahmadnagar.*

[17] *Or as the author grandiloquently expresses it: "The field of battle having been made dark as night by the clouds of dust his companions cast themselves like moths upon the flames of the fire-flashing swords."*

many of his men were killed. Raja Jai Singh and other rajas who were on another part of the hill, also joined in the fight. 'Azam Khan next came up in haste and ordered a part of the left wing to advance. At this time, when many of the Imperial officers had fallen, and the result seemed doubtful, the favour of Heaven fell upon the royal forces. The ill-starred Bahadur, observing the successive arrivals of reinforcements for his adversaries, lost heart, and turned to flee with his Afghans. His father also fled. As the discomfited rebels hurried down the hill, they were harassed by showers of arrows and bullets. A ball struck Bahadur Khan, and he was unable to continue his flight. Paras Ram, a servant of Raja Bihar Singh's, came up and despatched him with his dagger; then he cut off his head and sent it with his ring, horse and weapons, to Raja Bihar Singh, who forwarded them to 'Azam Khan. The Khan gave the horse to the man who had slain Bahadur, the ring he sent to the Emperor, and the head he caused to be set up as a warning over the gate of Bir.

The royal forces pursued the fugitives for three *kos,* and put many of them to the sword. But as the victors had been in the saddle from the first watch in the evening of one day to the third watch of the next day, and had marched more than thirty *kos,* men and beasts were both worn out, and were unable to go further. 'Azam Khan then called a halt, to allow of a little rest, and to give stragglers time to come up.

Khan-Jahan and his followers, whose horses were fresh, took advantage of this to improve their distance; but 'Azam Khan sent Muhammad Dakhni and the forces that were in Bir to maintain the pursuit, and he himself, after a brief interval, followed with the main force. When Khan-Jahan learnt that the victors were in full pursuit, he removed his ladies from the *howda* in which they had been carried by a female elephant, and mounting them on horses rode away with them. Darwesh Muhammad with a party of pursuers, captured the elephant and *howda,* and made a number of Afghans and their women prisoners. Most of Khan-Jahan's men who escaped were wounded, and in their panic they were able to carry off nothing but the clothes they wore and the horses they rode. Khan-Jahan, with a few faithful followers, escaped into the hill-country. . . . 'Azam Khan halted at Bir, to give his army a little rest. . . . Khan-Jahan then proceeded from Siu-ganw to Bizapur[18] and Bhonsla, in the Nizam-Shahi territory, with the design of going to Daulatabad. On hearing of this movement, 'Azam Khan marched from Bir towards Siu-ganw with 20,000 horse.

At this time, Sahu-ji Bhonsla, son-in-law of Jadu Rai, the Hindu commander of Nizam Shah's army, came in and joined 'Azam Khan. After the murder of Jadu Rai, which has been mentioned above, Sahu-ji broke off his connexion with Nizam Shah, and, retiring to the districts of Puna and Chakna, he wrote to 'Azam Khan, proposing to make his submission upon receiving a promise of protection. 'Azam Khan wrote to Court, and received orders to accept the proposal. Sahu-ji then came and joined him with two thousand horse. He received a *mansab* of 5,000,[19] a *khi'lat,* a gift of two *lacs* of rupees, and other presents. His brother Mina-ji received a robe and a *mansab* of 3,000 personal and 1,500 horse. Samaji son of Sahu-ji, also received a robe and a *mansab* of 2,000 personal and 1,000 horse. Several of their relations and dependents also obtained gifts and marks of distinction.

Khan-Jahan and Darya Khan, when they heard of the march of the Imperial forces towards Siu-ganw, quitted Bizapur and Bhonsla, and went to the village of Lasur, ten *kos* from Daulatabad. Nizam Shah also, on being informed of this advance, withdrew from Nizamā-

[18] *About 25 miles W. of Aurangabad.*

[19] "6,000 *Personal and* 5,000 *horse."—Khafi Khan.*

bad, which he had built outside of the fort of Daulatabad, and around which his adherents had built various houses and edifices, and entered into the fort itself. Khan-Jahan and Darya Khan, no longer deeming it safe to remain at Lasur, went to Ir-Kahtala, half a *kos* from Daulatabad, and few days later Khan-Jahan removed his family to Aubash-dara, a place within cover of Daulatabad. Darya Khan, with a thousand Afghans, separated from Khan-Jahan, marched towards Chandor, and the ghat of Chalis-ganw,[20] with the intention of attacking Andol and Dharan-Ganw.

This movement being reported to the Emperor,. . . he appointed 'Abdu-lla Khan, whom he had summoned from the Balaghat, to act against Darya Khan, and sent him off on the 10th Jumada-l awwal. Darya Khan had ravaged Andol, Dharanganw, and sundry other places of the Payin-ghat of Chalis-ganw; but on hearing of the approach of 'Abdulla Khan he turned back to the Balaghat. Want of rain and the ravages of the Nizam-Shahis and Afghans, had made provisions very scare about Daulatabad; so 'Azam Khan did not deem it prudent to advance in that direction, but thought it preferable to march against Mukarrab Khan and Bahlol, who were at Dharur and Ambajogai, in which plan of operations he was confirmed by a letter from Yaminu-d daula, who was at Ojhar. So he marched towards the ghat by way of Manik-dudh. (*After some fighting*) the royal forces ascended the ghat and took the village of Daman-ganw, twenty *kos* from Ahmadnagar. Next day they marched to Jamkhir,[21] in the Nizam-Shahi territories. . . . Leaving a force there, he next day proceeded to Tilangi. The garrison of the fort there had set in order, and opened fire upon him. . . . But in the course of one watch he took it by assault,

[20] *About 25 miles E. of Chandor, and the same N.W. of Aurangabad.*

[21] *About 30 miles S.E. of Aurangabad.*

2.

put many of the defenders to the sword, took nearly five hundred prisoners, and captured all the munitions of the fort. When the royal forces reached the banks of the Wanjara,[22] twelve *kos* from the fort of Dharur, they found that Mukarrab Khan and his confederates had passed down the pass of Anjan-dudh, and had gone to the neighbourhood of Bir. 'Azam Khan then sent Sahu-ji Bhonsla to take possession of the districts around Junir and Sangamnir, whilst he himself with the main force, went through the pass of Ailam to the town of Bir, and proceeded from thence to Partur, on the bank of the river Dudna. The enemy then fled towards Daulatabad. But 'Azam Khan learnt that scarcity of provisions prevented them from remaining in that vicinity and that they had moved off towards the Balaghat, by way of Dharur. He then determined to intercept and attack them. But he found that the enemy, having placed their elephants and beggage in the fort of Dharur, had the design of descending the Payin-ghat. So he went through the pass of Anjan-dudh, and encamped three *kos* from Dharur.

CAPTURE OF THE FORT OF MANSUR-GAR

In the course of the past year, Bakir Khan had proceeded to the pass of khera-para, two *kos* from Chhatardawar. This is a very narrow pass, between the territories of Kutbu-l Mulk and Orissa, and a small force of musketeers and archers might hold it in security. He ravaged the country round, but when the rains set in, he retired without making any attempt upon the fort of Mansur-garh which a slave of Kutbu-l Mulk's, named Mansur, had built about four *kos* from Khera-para. After the rains, under the royal orders, he again marched to Khera-para. Sher Muhammad, and other officers of Kutbu-l Mulk, had

[22] *Called in the maps "Manjira."*

collected about 3,000 horse and 10,000 foot, and having strengthened the fort with guns, muskets, and other implements of warfare, they made ready for battle. . . . On the 8th Jumada-l awwal, Bakir Khan arrived in the vicinity of Mansur-garh, and found the enemy drawn up in a plain north-east of the fort. . . . The enemy were unable to withstand the assault of the royal forces, but broke and fled. Flushed with victory, Bakir Khan resolved to attack the fort. Notwithstanding a heavy fire of cannons and muskets, he advanced to the base of the walls, planted his scaling-ladders, and began to ascend. The garrison being dismayed, took grass between their teeth, as is the manner of that country, and begged for quarter. Bakir Khan allowed them to march out in safety, and then placed a garrison of his own in the fort.

FLIGHT OF KHAN-JAHAN

The territories of Nizamu-l Mulk had suffered severely from the inroads of the Imperial forces in pursuit of Khan-Jahan, and mistrust and differences had arisen between the Nizam and Khan-Jahan; so the latter, in concert with Darya Khan, his chief adherents, and his remaining sons, resolved to retire to the Panjab, in order to seek the means of carrying on his insurrection among the disaffected Afghans of that country. So he left Daulatabad and proceeded towards Malwa. The Emperor, by his sagacity and foresight, had anticipated such a movement, and had sent 'Abdualla Khan to Malwa, in order to chastise Darya Khan. After Darya Khan had returned to the Balaghat, 'Abdulla Khan was directed to wait at the Payin-ghat, and to hasten after Darya Khan, whereever he might hear of him. Having got intelligence of his movements, 'Abdulla Khan went after him and reported the facts to the Court.

On the 24th Jumada-l awwal, the Emperor . . . appointed Saiyid Muzaffar Khan to support 'Abdu-lla

Khan, ... and on the 25th Rabiu-l awwal, he marched towards Malwa. He was directed to proceed by way of Bijagarh, and to cross the Nerbadda near Mandu. . . . If he found 'Abdu-lla Khan there, he was directed to join him. He marched with all speed, and crossed the Nerbadda at Akbarpur. 'Abdu-lla Khan having heard that Khan-Jahan had crossed at Dharampur,[23] he crossed the river at the same ford, and encamped at Lonihara. There he ascertained that on the 28th Jumada-l awwal, Khan-Jahan had moved off. He then proceeded to Dipalpur,[24] where he learnt that the rebels were plundering the neighbourhood of Ujjain, and he marched to Nulahi[25] in search of them.

FOURTH YEAR OF THE REIGN, 1040 A. H. (1630 A.D.)

Flight of Khan-Jahan

On the 4th, 'Abdu-lla Khan reached Nulahi, and Saiyid Muzaffar Khan, having left Dipalpur, reached Mankod on the 5th, on his way to Mandisor, when he learnt that the rebels had turned off to the right. On the 6th, he again marched and came to Talganw, and on that day 'Abdu-lla Khan came up from the rear and joined him. There they heard that the rebels were ten *kos* distant the day before, and had moved off that very morning. So they hastened off in pursuit. On the 10th they encamped at Khiljipur, and ascertained that the rebels were moving towards Sironj. The royal forces reached Sironj on the 14th and found that the rebels had come there two days previously. Khwaja Baba-e Aftab got into the city just before their arrival, and joining Khwaja 'Abdu-l Hadi, who was in the place, beat off the rebels, who only succeeded in carrying off fifty of the royal elephants.

[23] *S. W. of Mandu.*

[24] *Between Mandu and Ujjain.*

[25] *"Noulai" or "Nowlye," 60 miles N. of Mandu.*

BADSHAH-NAMA

Khan-Jahan and Darya Khan now found the roads closed on all sides against them. Every day that came they looked upon as their last, so in their despair they proceeded on the right from Sinroj, and entered the country of the Bundela, intending to push on to Kalpi, Jajhar Singh Bundela had incurred the royal censure because his son Bikramajit had allowed Khan-Jahan on his flight from Agra to pass through his territory and so reach the Dakhin. Bikramajit, to atone for his fault, and to remove the disgrace of his father, went in pursuit of the fugitives, and on the 17th came up with the rear-guard under Darya Khan, and attacked it with great vigour. That doomed one, under the intoxication of temerity or of wine, disdained to fly, and in his turn attacked. A musket-ball pierced his brainless skull, and his son was also killed. The Bundelas attacked him under the impression that he was Khan-Jahan, but that crafty one hastened from the field in another direction. Bikramajit cut off the head of Darya Khan, and also of his son, and sent them to Court, thus atoning for his former fault. Nearly four hundred Afghans and two hundred Bundelas were slain in the fight. For this service Bikramajit received the title of Jag-raj, and was advanced to the dignity of 2,000 personal and 2,000 horse.

CAPTURE OF THE FORT OF DHARUR

'Azam Khan, having ascended the pass of Anjan-dudh encamped three *kos* from Dharur. He then directed Multafit Khan and others to make an attack upon the town of Dharur and its *petta,* where once a week people from all parts, far and near, were accustomed to meet for buying and selling. The fort of Dharur was celebrated throughout the Dakhin for its strength and munitions of war. It was built upon the top of a ridge, and deep rivers of difficult passage ran on two sides of it. It was so secure that any effort upon it by the royal army was likely to prove unsuccessful; so Marhamat Khan was directed to plunder the town and *petta,* but not to make any attempt upon the fortress. . . . The garrison became disheartened, and remiss in their duty. . . . On the 23rd Jumada-s sani Marhamat Khan made his way in with a party of men, and opened the wicket. 'Azam Khan then entered with all his officers, and nearly two thousand men scaled the walls and got into the fort. All the vast munitions, the jewels, etc. became spoil of war.

DEATH OF KHAN-JAHAN LODI

The unhappy Khan-Jahan was greatly distressed and dismayed by the death of Darya Khan. Having no hope except in evasion, he fled and sought obscurity; but the royal forces pursued him closely. On the 28th Jumada-s sani, on arriving at the village of Nimi, in the country of Bhander,[26] the royal army learned that Khan-Jahan was about eight *kos* from that place. The long march they had made, and the company of many men who had been wounded in Jag-raj's action, prevented the royal forces from marching very early, but they drew near to the rebel.

Khan-Jahan, on hearing of their approach, sent off some of his Afghans, whose horses were knocked up, with the little baggage that was left; while he himself, with nearly a thousand horse, prepared to encounter Muzaffar Khan. The fight was sharp, great valour was exhibited, and many fell on both sides. . . . Khan-Jahan was wounded, his son Mahmud was killed with many of his followers, and further resistance was useless; so he again fled. Being hard pressed, he was every now and then

[26]*The text has Bandhu. Khafi Khan (vol. i. p. 40) calls it "Bhandur" but a MS. has Bhander, which is right. It lies N.E. of Jhansi.—Ain-i Akbari. vol. i. p.* 505.

obliged to abandon an elephant, so that before reaching Kalinjar twenty elephants had fallen into the hands of the pursuers, and some were caught by Raja Amar Singh Bandher. When Khan-Jahan approached Kalinjar, Saiyid Ahmad, the commandant of that fortress, came out to attack him. He killed several men, and took some prisoners. Hasan, another son of Khan-Jahan, was made prisoner; with him were captured twenty-two of the royal elephants, which Khan-Jahan had taken at Sironj. Khan-Jahan lost his *tugh* and banner, and fled with a handful of followers. By great exertion he travelled twenty *kos* that day, and reached the borders of Sahenda[27] where he was to end his mortal life. 'Abdu-lla Khan Bahadur and Saiyid Muzaffar Khan pursued him closely with their forces in array.

Khan-Jahan was much afflicted at the loss of his sons and faithful followers. All hope of escape was cut off; so he told his followers that he was weary of life, that he had reached the end of his career, and there was no longer any means of deliverance for him; he desired therefore, that every man should make off as best he could. A few determined to stand by him to the last, but many fled. The advanced forces of the royal army under Madhu Singh now came up. Khan-Jahan with his son 'Aziz, who was the dearest of all, and Aimal, and the Afghans, who remained constant, placed their two remaining elephants in front, and advanced to meet Muzaffar Khan. They made their charge, and when Khan-Jahan found that they were determined to take him, he alighted from his horse and fought desparately. In the midst of the struggle Madhu Singh pierced him with a spear, and before Muzaffar Khan could come up

[27]*"The tank of Sindraha."—Khafi Khan, vol. i. p.* 44. *Blochmann gives the name as "Sehonda." It lies north of Kalinjar on the Ken.—Ain-i Akbari, vol. i. p* 505.

the brave fellows cut Khan-Jahan. his dear son 'Aziz and Aimal, to pieces. About a hundred of his adherents fell, and their heads were cut off, but a party escaped. A grandson of Saiyid Muzaffar Khan and twenty-seven other royalists were slain. The heads of Khan-Jahan, 'Aziz and Aimal were sent to the Imperial Court. Farid, a son of Khan-Jahan, was taken and placed in confinement. Another son, named Jan-i Jahan, had fled and taken refuge in Sahenda with the mother of Bahadur Khan. 'Abdu-lla Khan sent for him, and then despatched him in custody to Court. . . . The heads of the rebels were placed over the gate of the fort. After their victory, 'Abdu-lla Khan and Saiyid Muzaffar Khan came to Court, and received many marks of favour. The former was advanced to a *mansab* of 6,000 and 6,000 horse, and he received the title Firoz-Jang. Saiyid Muzaffar Khan was promoted to a *mansab* of 5,000 and 5,000 horse. He received the title Khan-Jahan.

ATTACK ON PARENDA

'Azam Khan was in the neighbourhood of Parenda,[28] intent upon the reduction of that fortress, and the capture of the elephants and stores which had been sent there. . . . He sent Raja Jai Singh with a detachment to ravage the town and *petta*: The Raja first plundered the *petta,* which was about a *kos* distant on the left of the fortress. He then attacked the town, which was surrounded by a mud (*kham*) wall five *gaz* high and three *gaz* thick, and by a ditch of three cubits (*sih zara'*) broad (?). He broke through the walls by means of his elephants, and the musketeers of the garrison then fled into the ditch of the fort. The town was plundered. 'Azam Khan then arrived, . . . and

[28]*Near the Sina river on the route from Ahmadnagar to Sholapur. It is about sixty miles S. W. of Dharur.*

entered the town, to secure the elephants belonging to the enemy, which had been taken into the ditch of the fortress. Seven elephants were seized and brought out, and much other booty was secured. . . . 'Azam Khan pressed the siege, and the troops drove zigzags[29] up to the edge of the ditch in three places, and began to fill it up. He raised a battery exactly opposite the gate of the fortress, at the distance of an arrow-shot from the moat. He then pushed his zigzags to the very edge of the moat, and there raised a battery, to which the men in the Sher-Haji[30] found it very difficult to reply.

It now became evident that 'Adil Khan, through his tender years, had no real power, but that the reins of government were in the hands of a slave named Daulat, who had been originally a minstrel (*kulawant*), and whom the King's father, Ibrahim 'Adil, had ennobled with the title of Daulat Khan, and had placed in command of the fortress of Bijapur. This ungrateful infamous fellow, after the death of Ibrahim, assumed the title "Khawass Khan," and delivered the government over to a mischievous turbulent *brahman*, named Murari Pandit. This same Daulat put out the eyes of Darwesh Muhammad, the eldest son of Ibrahim 'Adil Khan by the daughter of Kutbu-l Mulk, and demanded his daughter in marriage, thus bringing to infamy the name and honour of his indulgent patron. The 'Adil-Khanis and the Nizam-Shahis had now made common cause and were united.

The siege of Parenda had gone on for a month. Provender had throughout been difficult to procure, and now no grass was to be found within twenty *kos*. So

[29] *"Kucha-e salamat," ways of safety.*

[30] *This is not a proper name. There was a Sher-Haji also at Kandahar, and at many other places. It is apparently an advanced work, and probably bears the name of its inventor.*

'ABDU-L HAMID LAHORI

'Azam Khan was obliged to raise the siege, and to go to Dharur. . . . The 'Adil-Khanis retreated before 'Azam Khan, and he encamped on the banks of the Wanjira. Next day he captured the town and fort of Balni, which the inhabitants defended in the hope of receiving assistance. After plundering the place, he marched to Mandu[31] and from Mandu to Dharur.

FAMINE IN THE DAKHIN AND GUJARAT

. During the past year no rain had fallen in the territories of the Balaghat, and the drought had been especially severe about Daulatabad. In the present year also there had been a deficiency in the bordering countries, and a total want in the Dakhin and Gujarat. The inhabitants of these two countries were reduced to the direst extremity. Life was offered for a loaf,[32] but none would buy; rank was to be sold for a cake, but none cared for it; the ever-bounteous hand was now stretched out to beg for food; and the feet which had always trodden the way of contentment walked about only in search of sustenance. For a long time dog's flesh was sold for goat's flesh, and the pounded bones of the dead were mixed with flour and sold. When this was discovered, the sellers were brought to justice. Destitution at length reached such a pitch that men began to devour each other, and the flesh of a son was preferred to his love. The numbers of the dying caused obstructions in the roads, and every man whose dire sufferings did not terminate in death and who retained the power to move wandered off to the towns and villages of other countries. Those lands which had been famous for their fertility and plenty now retained no trace of productiveness. . . . The Emperor in his gracious

[31]*So in the text; but the maps give no such name between Parenda and Dharur.*

[32]*"Jane ba nane."*

kindness and bounty directed the officials of Burhanpur, Ahmadabad, and the country of Surat, to establish soup kitchens, or alms-houses, such as are called *langer* in the language of Hindustan, for the benefit of the poor and destitute. Every day sufficient soup and bread was prepared to satisfy the wants of the hungry. It was further ordered that so long as His Majesty remained at Burhanpur 5,000 rupees should be distributed among the deserving poor every Monday, that day being distinguished above all others as the day of the Emperor's accession to the throne. Thus, on twenty Mondays one *lac* of rupees was given away in charity. Ahmadabad had suffered more severely than any other place, and so His Majesty ordered the officials to distribute 50,000 rupees among the famine-stricken people. Want of rain and dearness of grain had caused great distress in many other countries. So under the directions of the wise and generous Emperor taxes amounting to nearly seventy *lacs* of rupees were remitted by the revenue officers—a sum amounting to nearly eighty *krors* of *dams,* and amounting to one-eleventh part of the whole revenue. When such remissions were made from the exchequer. it may be conceived how great were the reductions made by the nobles who held *jagirs* and *mansabs.*

CAPTURE OF THE FORT OF SITUNDA

——— Siphadar Khan, after obtaining possession of the fort of Taltam (by the treachery of the garrison), laid seige to Situnda[33] by command of the Emperior, and pressed the place very hard. Sidi Jamal, the governor, offered to surrender on terms which were agreed to; so he and his family came out, and the fort passed into the possession of the Imperialists.

CAPTURE OF KANDAHAR

(p. 374). Nasiri Khan had been placed in command of

[33] *About fifty miles N. E. from Aurangabad.*

a force, with instructions to conquer the kingdom of Telingana. He resolved upon reducing the fort of Kandahar,[34] which was exceedingly strong, and the most famous one of that country. It was under the command of Sadik, the son of Yakut Khudawand Khan, and was in full state of preparation. On the 23rd Jumada-l awwal he encamped one *kos* from the fortress. Next day he prepared to attack the town of Kandahar; but before reaching the place he was opposed by Sarfaraz Khan, the general commanding in that country, who had taken up a position between the fort and the town, and having covered his front with artillery, awaited the attack. He was protected also by the guns and muskets of the fortress. The royal army attacked with great vigour, and killed a great many of the enemy. Sarfaraz Khan with a few followers fled to the Nizam-Shahis. After this Nasiri Khan pushed on the siege. . . . Randaula, Mukarrab Khan, and others, with a united force of 'Adil-Khanis and Nizam-Shahis, camp up to attack him in his trenches. Undismayed by this fresh enemy, he boldly faced his assailants; and although he had also to bear the fire of the guns and muskets of the fortress, he defeated them with considerable loss, and compelled them to fall back a distance of three *kos*.

Out of twenty-one mines which had been opened, six were complete; three were charged with powder, and three were kept in reserve. 'Azam Khan, who had marched to support Nasiri Khan, now approached, and Nasiri Khan went forth to meet him, and to bring him to see the springing of the mines and the assault upon the fortress. The match was applied to the three mines: one failed, but the other two brought down the wall of the Sher-Haji with half a bastion. The garrison kept up a discharge of rockets, mortars, stones and grenades.

[34]*About seventy-five miles E. of Dharur, and twenty-five S. W. of Nander.*

but the storming parties pressed on. The conflict raged from mid-day till sunset, but the wall of the fortress was not sufficiently levelled, and the defenders kept up such a heavy fire that the assailants were forced to retire. At night the trenches were carried forward, and preparations were made for firing the other mines. The garrison saw that the place must fall, and . . . . made offers of surrender, which were accepted and the Imperial troops took possession of the fortress. . . . The siege had lasted four months and nineteen days, and the place fell on the 15th Shawwal.

DEATH OF THE QUEEN 'ALIYA BEGAM

On the 17th Zi-l ka'da, 1040, died Nawab 'Aliya Begam,[35] in the fortieth year of her age, to the great grief of her husband the Emperor. . . . She had borne him eight sons and six daughters. The third child and eldest son was Muhammad Dara Shukoh, the forth Muhammad Shah Shuja, the sixth Muhammad Aurangzeb, the tenth Murad Bakhsh.

NIZAM SHAH

(p. 395). A letter from Sipahdar Khan informed the Emperor how Fath Khan, feeling that his release from confinement by Nizam Shah had been a matter of necessity, and that he would be imprisoned again as soon as his master's mind was at ease, he had resolved to be beforehand with him, and had placed Nizam Shah in confinement, as his faher Malik 'Ambar had done before. . . . Fath Khan then addressed a letter to Yaminu-d daula Asaf Khan, informing him that he had placed Nizam Shah in confinement on account of his evil character and his enmity to the Imperial throne, for which act he hoped to receive some mark of favour.

[35]*Otherwise called "Mumtaz Mahal." She died in childbirth—Khafi Khan, vol. i. p.* 459.

In answer he was told that if he wished to prove his sincerity, he should rid the world of such a worthless and wicked being. On receiving this direction, Fath Khan secretly made away with Nizam Shah, but gave out that he had died a natural death. He placed Nizam Shah's son Husain, a lad of ten years old, on the throne as his successor. He reported these facts to the Imperial Court, and was directed to send the jewels and valuables of the late king, and his own eldest son as a hostage.

OPERATIONS AGAINST 'ADIL KHAN

. Muhammad 'Adil Khan (of Bijapur), through youth, inexperience, and evil counsellors, especially a slave named Daulat (who had assumed the title of Khawase Khan), had shown himself unfaithful to the Imperial throne, and regardless of the allegiance paid by his father. The Emperor commissioned Yaminu-d daula Asaf Khan to arouse him from his negligence and disregard of his duty. Asaf Khan was empowered to demand from him a return to obedience and the payment of tribute.[36] If he agreed to those terms, he was to be left alone; if not, as much as possible of his territory was to be conquered, and the rest laid waste.

FIFTH YEAR OF THE REIGN, 1041 A.H. (1631 A.D.)

Campaign against Bijapur

Asaf Khan proceeded on his expedition, and arrived at Nander, where he remained two days. There he left the main part of his army, and proceeded express to the fort of Kandahar, which he inspected. One stage further on he came to the fort of Bhalki.[37] . . . Orders were given for the reduction of the place, and entrenchments were commenced, but it was resolved to attempt

[36] *The Shah-Jahan-nama says that the surrender of the fort of Parenda was to be also required.*

[37] *Twenty-fives miles N. W. of Bidr.*

the capture of the place by escalade at night. The garrison got notice of this, and evacuated the place under cover of darkness. . . . Asaf Khan then marched towards Kalanor, a flourishing place belonging to 'Adil Khan. When he arrived at Sultanpur, near the city of Kulbarga, the general in command had taken the principal inhabitants into the fort of Kulbarga, which was well armed with guns, muskets, and other instruments of war. Next day 'Azam Khan, under the directions of Asaf Khan, made an attack upon the town, and caried it, notwithstanding a heavy fire from the fort.

The victors plundered whatever they could lay their hands on, and captured many horses in the ditch of the fortress. Asaf Khan did not deem it expedient to attempt the reduction of the fortress, as it would have been a difficult undertaking and a cause of delay; so he retired, and encamped near the river Nahnura. Then he advanced to the vicinity of Bijapur, and encamped on the borders of a tank between Nauras-pur[38] and Shahpur. The enemy every day came out of the ditch into the plain, and there was a warm interchange of rockets, arrows, and musketry. But although the enemy kept up also a heavy fire from the fortifications, they were regularly driven back to the shelter of the walls.

Asaf Khan used to take every precaution for the safety of the detachments which went out every day to collect fodder, but the army was large and the animals numerous, so this was no easy matter.

The enemy were constantly on the alert, and struck whenever they got an opportunity. . . . At the beginning a man named Shaikh Dabir, one of the confidants of Khawass Khan, came out with overtures of peace and offers of tribute; but as they were not worthy of trust, they were rejected. Afterwards Mustafa Khan, son-in-

[38]*The text has "Nur-siyur," but the index of Names corrects it.*

law of Mulla Muhammad Lahori, kept up a secret correspondence with Asaf Khan, expressing his devotion and proposing to admit the Imperial troops into the fortress. . . . After much negotiation, it was agreed that Mustafa Khan and Khairiyat Khan Habshi, uncle of Randaula, should come to Asaf Khan and arrange for the transmission of tribute and the settlement of the terms of peace. Accordingly both came out of Bijapur . . . . and it was finally agreed that 'Adil Khan should send tribute to the value of forty *lacs* of rupees in jewels. valuables, elephants, and money, and that he should ever after remain faithful to his allegiance. A treaty in these terms was accordingly drawn up. . . . The two negotiators returned to Bijapur, and Shaikh 'Abdu-r Rahim Khairabadi went in with them to obtain 'Adil Khan's signature to the treaty.

On the third day the Shaikh was sent back with a message that they would send out their own *wakils* with the treaty. Next day the came out with certain propositions that Asaf Khan considered reasonable, and he accepted them. It was agreed that the treaty should be sent out next day. As they were about to depart, one of the *wakils,* who was a confidant of Mustafa Khan, dropped a letter of his before Asaf Khan without the knowledge of his companion. The letter said that Khawass Khan was well aware that provender was very scarce in the Imperial army; that the fetching of grass and fuel from long distances was a work of great toil to man and beast; and that in consequence it would be impossible for the Imperial army to maintain its position more than a few days longer. Khawass Khan had therefore resolved to have recourse to artifice and procrastination, in the expectation that Asaf Khan would be obliged to raise the siege and retire baffled.

The siege had lasted twenty days, and during that time no corn had reached the army, and before its arrival the enemy had laid waste all the country round and carried off the grain to distant places. The provisions which the army had brought with it were all exhausted, and grain had risen to the price of one rupee per *sir*. Men and beasts were sinking. So it was resolved, after consultation, that the royal army should remove from Bijapur into some better supplied part of the enemy's country, that the Imperial army might be recruited, and the territory of the enemy be wasted at the same time. With this intention the royal army marched along the bank of the Kishan Gang[39] to Raibagh and Miraj,[40] two of the richest places in that country. Wherever they found supplies they rested, and parties were sent out to plunder in all directions. On whatever road they went they killed and made prisoners, and ravaged and laid waste on both sides. From the time of their entering the territories to the time of their departure they kept up this devastation and plunder. The best part of the country was trodden under, and so, the forces had recovered strength and the rains were near, the royal army passed by the fort of Sholapur, and descended by the passes into the Imperial territories. 15,000 men of the enemy, who had followed them to Sholapur, then turned back to Bijapur.

RETURN OF THE COURT FROM BURHANPUR TO AGRA

(Text. vol. i. p. 421). The Emperor being tired of his residence at Burhanpur, resolved to return to the capital; so he set out on the 24th Ramazan, . . . and arrived there on the 1st Zi-l hijja, 1041 A.H.

Affairs in the Dakhin had not been managed so well as they ought to have been by 'Azam Khan; so a mandate

[39]*The Kistna or Krishna.*

[40]*Miraj is on the left bank of the Kistna, about thirty miles E. of Kolapur. Raibagh is about twenty-five miles lower to the S.E., and on the other side of the river.*

was sent to Mahabat Khan Khan-khanan, informing him that the government of Khandesh and the Dakhin had been conferred upon him, and he was directed to make the necessary preparations as quickly as possible. and start from Dehli to meet the Emperor and receive instructions. Yaminu-d daula Asaf Khan, with 'Azam Khan and other nobles under his command, were directed to return to Court.

CAPTURE OF THE PORT OF HUGLI

(p. 434). Under the rule of the Bengalis (*dar'ahdi Bangaliyan*) a party of Frank merchants, who are inhabitants of Sundip, came trading to Satganw. One *kos* above that place, they occupied some ground on the bank of the estuary.[41] Under the pretence that a building was necessary for their transactions in buying and selling, they erected several houses in the Bengali style. In course of time, through the ignorance and negligence of the rulers of Bengal, these Europeans increased in number, and erected large substantial buildings, which they fortified with cannons, muskets, and other implements of war. In due course, a considerable place grew up, which was known by the name of the Port of Hugli. On one side of it was the river, and on the other three sides was a ditch filled from the river. European ships used to go up to the port, and a trade was established there. The markets of Satganw declined and lost their prosperity. The villages and districts of Hugli were on both sides of the river, and these the Europeans got possession of at a low rent. Some of the inhabitants by force, and more by hopes of gain, they infected with their Nazarene teaching, and sent them off in ships to Europe. In the hope of an everlasting reward, but in reality of an exquisite torture, they consoled themselves with

[41] *The word used is khur, "an estuary," here apparently meaning a tidal river.*

the profits of their trade for the loss of rent which arose from the removal of the cultivators. These hateful practices were not confined to the lands they occupied, but they seized and carried off every one they could lay their hands upon along the sides of the river.

These proceedings had come under the notice of the Emperor before his accession, . . . and he resolved to put an end to them if ever he ascended the throne, that the coinage might always bear the stamp of the glorious dynasty, and the pulpit might be graced with its *khutba*. After his accession, he appointed Kasim Khan to the government of Bengal, and . . . impressed upon him the duty of overthrowing these mischievous people. He was ordered, as soon as he attended to the necessary duties of his extensive province, to set about the extermination of the pernicious intruders. Troops were to be sent both by water and land, so that this difficult enterprise might be quickly and easily accomplished.

Kasim Khan set about making his preparations, and at the close of the cold season, in Sha'ban, 1040 A.H., he sent his son 'Inayatu-ulla with Allah Yar Khan, who was to be the real commander of the army, and several other nobles, to effect the conquest of Hugli. He also sent Bahadur Kambu, an active and intelligent servant of his, with the force under his command, under the pretence of taking possession of the *Khalisa* lands at Makhsusabad, but really to join Allah Yar Khan at the proper time. Under the apprehension that the infidels, upon getting intelligence of the march of the armies, would put their families on board ships, and so escape from destruction to the disappointment of the warriors of Islam, it was given out that the forces were marching to attack Hijli. Accordingly it was arranged that Allah Yar Khan should halt at Bardwan, which lies in the direction of Hijli, until he received intelligence of Khwaja Sher and others, who had been ordered to proceed in boats from Sripur[42] to cut off the retreat of the Firingis. When the flotilla arrived at Mohana, which is a *dahna*[43] of the Hugli, Allah Yar Khan was to march with all expedition from Bardwan to Hugli, and fall upon the infidels. Upon being informed that Khwaja Sher and his companions had arrived at the *dahna*, Allah Yar Khan made a forced march from Bardwan, and in a night and day reached the village of Haldipur, between Satganw and Hugli. At the same time he was joined by Bahadur Kambu, who arrived from Makhsusabad, with 500 horse and a large force of infantry. Then he hastened to the place where Khwaja Sher had brought the boats, and between Hugli and the sea, in a narrow part of the river, he formed a bridge of boats so that ships could not get down to the sea; thus the flight of the enemy was prevented.

On the 2nd Zi-l hijja, 1041, the attack was made on the Firingis by the boatmen on the river, and by the forces on land. An inhabited place outside of the ditch was taken and plundered, and the occupants were slain. Detachments were then ordered to the villages and places on both sides of the river, so that all the Christians found there might be sent to hell. Having killed or captured all the infidels, the warriors carried off the families of their boatmen, who were all Bengalis. Four thousand boatmen, whom the Bengalis called *ghrabi*, then left the Firingis and joined the victorious army. This was a great discouragement to the Christians.

The royal army was engaged for three months and a half in the siege of this strong place. Sometimes the infidels fought, sometimes they made overtures of peace, protracting the time in hopes of succour from their countrymen. With base treachery they pretended to make proposals of peace, and sent nearly a lac of rupees

[42] *Serampore.*

[43] *Qy. Bengali dahra, a lake,*

as tribute, while at the same time they ordered 7,000 musketeers who were in their service to open fire. So heavy was it that many of the trees of a grove in which a large force of the besiegers was posted were stripped of their branches and leaves.

At length the besiegers sent their pioneers to work upon the ditch, just by the church, where it was not so broad and deep as elsewhere. There they dug channels and drew off the water. Mines were then driven on from the trenches, but two of these were discovered by the enemy and counteracted. The centre mine was carried under an edifice which was loftier and stronger than all the other buildings, and where a large number of Firingis were stationed. This was charged and tamped. On the 14th Rabi'u-l awwal the besieger's forces were drawn up in front of this building, in order to allure the enemy to that part. When a large number were assembled, a heavy fire was opened; and the mine was fired. The building was blown up, and the many infidels who had collected around it were sent flying into the air. The warriors of Islam rushed to the assault. Some of the infidels found their way to hell by the water. but some thousands succeeded in making their way to the ships. At this juncture Khwaja Sher came up with the boats. and killed many of the fugitives.

These foes of the faith were afraid lest one large ship, which had nearly two thousand men and women and much property on board, should fall into the hands of the Muhammadans; so they fired the magazine and blew her up. Many others who were on board the *gharbs* set fire to their vessels, and turned their faces towards hell. Out of the sixty-four large *dingas*, fifty-seven *ghrabs* and 200 *jaliyas*, one *ghrab* and two *jaliyas* escaped, in consequence of some fire from the burning ships having fallen upon some boats laden with oil, which burnt a way through (the bridge of boats). Whoever escaped from the water and fire became a prisoner.

From the beginning of the siege to the conclusion, men and women, old and young, altogether nearly 10,000 of the enemy were killed, being either blown up with powder, drowned in water, or burnt by fire. Nearly 1,000 brave warriors of the Imperial army obtained the glory of martyrdom. 4,400 Christians of both sexes were taken prisoners, and nearly 10,000 inhabitants of the neighbouring country who had been kept in confinement by these tyrants were set at liberty.

SURRENDER OF THE FORT OF GALNA

(Text, vol. i. p. 442.) After Fath Khan, son of Malik 'Ambar, had put Nizam Shah to death, Mahmud Khan, the commandant of the fort of Galna, repudiated his authority, and put the fortress in a state of defence, intending to deliver it over to Sahu-ji Bhonsla, who, unmindful of the favours he had received from the Imperial throne, had strayed from the path of obedience, and had possessed himself of Nasik, Trimbak, Sangamnir and Junir, as far as the country of Kokan. He had got into his power one of the relatives of the late Nizam Shah, who had been confined in one of the strongest fortresses in the kingdom, and raised the banner of independence. He (Mahmud Khan)[44] wished to deliver the fort over to him. Khan-zaman, who was acting as deputy of his father in the government of the Dakhin, Birar and Khandesh, when he was informed of Mahmud Khan's proceedings, wrote to Mir Kasim Khan Harawi, commandant of the fort of Alang, which is near to Galna. He directed him to endeavour by promises of Imperial favour to win him over, and prevent the surrender of the fortress to Sahu-ji Bhonsla. Mir Kasim communicated with Mahmud Khan on the subject, and the latter invited the Mir to come to him. After a good

[44]*This seems to be the sense of the passage, but it is obscure.*

deal of talk, Mahmud Khan assented to the position, and in the hope of a great reward delivered over the fort to the representatives of the Emperor.

SIXTH YEAR OF THE REIGN, 1042 A.H. (1632 A.D.)

(Text, vol. i. p. 449). Bhagirat Bhil, chief of the disaffected in the province of Malwa, relying on the number of his followers and the strength of his fort of Khatakhiri,[45] had refused obedience to the governors of Malwa. He ventured to show his disaffection to Nusrat Khan, when he was governor, and the Khan marched from Sarangpur to chastise him. The Khan's fame as a soldier had its effect. The rebel gave up all hope of resistance, and, seeking an introduction to Nusrat Khan through Sangram, Zamindar of Kanur, he surrendered his fortress.

DESTRUCTION OF HINDU TEMPLES

(p. 449.) It had been brought to the notice of His Majesty that during the late reign many idol temples had been begun, but remained unfinished, at Benares, the great stronghold of infidelity. The infidels were now desirous of completing them. His Majesty, the defender of the faith, gave orders that at Benares, and throughout all his dominions in every place, all temples that had been begun should be cast down. It was now reported from the province of Allahabad that seventy-six temples had been destroyed in the district of Benares.

CONQUEST OF DAULATABAD

(p. 496). Fath Khan, son of 'Ambar Habshi, conceiving his interest to lie in making submission to the Emperor, had sent his son, 'Abdu-r Rusul, with a suitable offering to the foot of that Imperial throne, professing obedience and praying for favour. The Emperor graci-

[45] *"Kuntharkera," in Malcolm's Map of Central India, on the Kali Sind, about thirty miles N. of Ujjain.*

ously bestowed upon him some districts which had formerly belonged to him, but had been since given to Sahu-ji Bhonsla. Now, in compliance with the request of Fath Khan, they were restored to him. This gave great offence to the turbulent Sahu-ji, who went and joined the Bijapuris, and induced 'Adil Khan to place him in command of a force for wresting the fortress of Daulatabad from the hands of Fath Khan. The latter was much incensed against the Nizam-Shahis, and had no faith in them; so he wrote to Khan-khanan Mahabat Khan, informing him that Sahu-ji Bhonsla was preparing to bring a force from Bijapur against him, and that, as the fortress was ill provisioned, there was great probability of its being taken, unless Mahabat Khan came to his assistance. If the Khan came quickly, he would surrender the fortress, and would himself proceed to the Imperial Court. The Khan-khanan accordingly sent forward his son, Khan-zaman, with an advanced force, and he himself followed on the 9th Jumada-s sani. *(Khan-zaman defeats a covering army of Bijapur)*.

The Bijapuris were discouraged by the chastisement they had received from the Imperial army, so they made offers of an arrangement to Fath Khan. They offered to leave the fortress in his possession, to give him three *lacs* of *pagodas* in cash, and to throw provisions into the fort. That ill-starred foolish fellow, allured by these promises, broke his former engagement, and entered into an alliance with them. Most of the animals in the fortress had died from want of provender, and the Bijapuris now, at the instance of Fath Khan, exerted themselves in getting provisions. When Khan-khanan, who was at Zafarnagar, was informed of these proceedings, he wrote to Khan-zaman directing him to make every exertion for the reduction of the fortress, and for the punishment of the traitor and the Bijapuris. *(Skirmishes in the vicinity)*.

Khan-khanan, on being informed of the state of

affairs, marched from Zafarnagar to Daulatabad. and reached there on the last day of Sha'ban. Next morning rode out with his son, Khan-zaman, to reconnoitre the fortress, and took up his residence in a house belonging to Nizam Shah at Nizampur, near the fortress. (*Disposition of his forces.*) He placed the artillery and siege material under the direction of (his son) Luhrasp, and ordered that a constant fire should be kept up from a high hill which governs the fortress, and upon which Kaghziwara stands. He also ordered Khan-zaman to be constantly on the alert with 5,000 cavalry, and ready to render assistance wherever it might be required in the trenches. The Imperial army having thus invested the place, and formed trenches, pushed on the siege, running zigzags, forming mines and preparing scaling ladders.

Fath Khan placed the son of Nizam Shah in the Kala-kot (black fort), which was considered impregnable. He himself took post in the Maha-kot (great port), and the body of the forces were stationed in the outer works called 'Ambar-kot, because they had been raised by Malik 'Ambar to protect the place against the advance of the Imperial power. (*Defeat of many attempts to victual and relieve the fortress from without, and of sorties from within.*)

On the 9th Shawwal a mine which had been formed from the trenches of Khan-zaman was charged, and the forces having been named for the assault, were ordered to assemble in the trenches before break of day. The mine was to be fired at the first appearance of dawn, and upon the walls being blown down, the stormers were to rush into the fort. By mistake the mine was fired an hour before dawn, and before the storming parties were ready. Twenty-eight *gaz* of the walls and twelve *gaz* of the bastion was blown away, and a wide breach was made. But the troops not having arrived, no entry was effected. The defenders rushed to the breach, and kept up such a rain of arrows, bullets, and rockets, that the storming party was obliged to take refuge in the trenches. Then they exerted themselves to stop the breach with palisades and planks. The commander of the Imperial army desired to dismount and lead the assult, but Nasiri Khan urged that it was against all the rules of warfare for the commander-in-chief to act in such a way. He himself would lead the storming party, trusting in God and hoping for the favour of the Emperor. Khan-khanan directed Mahes Das Rathor and others to support him. The Imperial troops rushed to the breach, and the defenders made a desperate resistance; but Nasiri Khan, although wounded, forced his way in upon the right, and Raja Bihar Singh and other Hindus upon the left. They were fiercely encountered by Khairiyat Khan Bijapuri and others with sword and dagger, but they at length prevailed, and drove the defenders into the ditch of the Maha-kot for shelter. Great numbers of the garrison fell under the swords of the victors. Thus fell the celebrated works of Malik 'Ambar, which were fourteen *gaz* in height and ten *gaz* in thickness, and well furnished with guns and all kinds of defences. The Imperial commander having thus achieved a great success, proceeded with Nasiri Khan to inspect the works, and immediately took steps for attacking the Maha-kot. *(Diversion made by the enemy in the direction of Birar. Another attempt by Randaula and Sahu-ji to relieve the fortress.)*

With great perseverance the besiegers pushed a mine under the Maha-kot, and Fath Khan was so much alarmed that he sent his wives and family into the Kala-kot. He himself, with Khairiyat Khan, uncle of Randaula, and some other Bijapuris, remained in the Maha-kot. The Bijapuris being greatly depressed by the scarcity of food and the progress of the Imperial arms, sought permission through Malu-ji to be allowed to escape secretly, and to go to their master. Khan-khanan sent a written consent, and by kind words encouraged their drooping spirits. Nearly two hundred of them after nightfall descended by a ladder fastened to the battlements. Khan-khanan sent for them, and consoled them with kind words and presents. (*Several more attempts to relieve the fortress*).

On the 25th Zi-l ka'da, the commander-in-chief visited the trenches. He went to Saiyid 'Alawal, whose post was near the mine of the Sher-Haji of the Maha-kot, and determined that the mine should be blown up. Fath Khan got notice of this, and in the extremity of his fear he sent his *wakil* to Khan-khanan, and with great humility represented that he had bound himself to the 'Adil-Khanis by the most solemn compact not to make peace without their approval. He therefore wished to send one of his followers to Murari Pandit, to let him know how destitute the fort was of provisions, and how hard it was pressed by the besiegers. He also wanted the Pandit to send *wakils* to settle with him the terms of peace and the surrender of the fort. He therefore begged that the explosion of the mine might be deferred for that day, so that there might be time for an answer to come from Murari Pandit. Khan-khanan knew very well that there was no sincerity in his proposal, and that he only wanted to gain a day by artifice; so he replied that if Fath Khan wished to delay the explosion for a day, he must immediately send out his son as a hostage.

When it had become evident that Fath Khan did not intend to send his son out, the mine was exploded. A bastion and fifteen yards of the wall were blown up. The brave men who awaited the explosion rushed forward, and heedless of the fire from all sorts of arms which fell upon them from the top of the Maha-kot, they made their way in. The commander-in-chief now directed that Saiyid 'Alawal and others who held the trenches on the outside of the ditch, opposide the Sher-

Haji, should go inside and bravely cast up trenches in the interior. (*Defeat of a demonstration made by Murari Pandit. Surrender of the fort of Nabati near Galna*).

Fath Khan now woke up from his sleep of heedlessness and security. He saw that Daulatabad could not resist the Imperial arms and the vigour of the Imperial commander. To save the honour of his own and Nizam Shah's women, he sent his eldest son 'Abdu-r Rusul to Khan-khanan, (*laying the blame of his conduct on Sahu-ji and 'Adil-Khanis*). He begged for forgiveness and for a week's delay, to enable him to remove his and Nizam Shah's family from the fortress, while his son remained as a hostage in Khan-khanan's power. Khan-khanan had compassion on his fallen condition, granted him safety, and kept his son as a hostage. Fath Khan asked to be supplied with the means of carrying out his family and property, and with money for expenses. Khan-khanan sent him his own elephants and camels and several litters also ten *lacs* and fifty thousand rupees in cash, belonging to the State, and demanded the surrender of the fortress. Fath Khan sent the keys to Khan-khanan, and set about preparing for his own departure. Khan-khanan then placed trusty guards over the gates.

On the 19th Zi-l hijja Fath Khan came out of the fortress and delivered it up. The fortress consisted of nine different works, five upon the low ground, and four upon the top of the hill. These with the guns and all the munitions of war were surrendered Khan-khanan went into the fortress, and had the *kutba* read in the Emperor's name.

The old name of the fortress of Daulatabad was Deo-gir, or Dharagar. It stands upon a rock with towers to the sky. In circumference it measures 5000 legal *gaz*, and the rock all round is scarped so carefully, from the base of the fort to the level of water, that a snake or an ant would ascend it with difficulty. Around it there is a moat forty legal yards (*zara'*) in width, and thirty in depth, cut into the solid rock. In the heart of the rock there is a dark and tortuous passage, like the ascent of a minaret, and a light is required there in broad daylight. The steps are cut in the rock itself, and the bottom is closed by an iron gate. It is by this road and way that the fortress is entered. By the passage a large iron brazier had been constructed, which, when necessary, could be placed in the middle of it, and a fire being kindled in this brazier, its heat would effectually prevent all progress. The ordinary means of besieging a fort by mines, *sabats,* etc., are of no avail against it. . .

Khan-khanan desired to leave a garrison in the captured fortress, and to go to Burhanpur, taking Nizam Shah and Fath Khan with him. The Imperial army had endured many hardships and privations during the siege. They had continually to contend against 20,000 horse of Bijapur and Nizamu-l Mulk, and to struggle hard for supplies. Nasiri Khan (who had been created Khan-dauran) was always ready for service, and he offered to take the command of the fortress. So Khan-khanan left him and some other officers in change, and marched with his army to Zafarnagar. . . . After reaching that place, Murari Pandit and the Bijapuris sent Farhad, the father of Randaula, to treat for peace; but Khan-khanan knew their artfulness and perfidy, and sent him back again. The Bijapuris, in despair and recklessness, now turned back to Daulatabad. They knew that provisions were very scarce and the garrison small. The entrenchments which the besiegers had raised were not thrown down, so the Bijapuris took possession of them, invested the fortress and fought against it. Khan-dauran, without waiting for reinforcements, boldly sallied out and attacked them repeatedly. By kind treatment he had conciliated the *raiyats* of the neighbourhood, and they supplied him with provisions, so that he was in no want. As soon as Khan-khanan heard of these proceedings he marched for Daulatabad. The enemy finding that they could accomplish nothing, abandoned the siege as soon as they heard of the approach of Khan-khanan, and then retreated by Nasik and Trimbak.

CHRISTIAN PRISONERS

(Text, vol.i.p.534) on the 11th Muharram, (1043 A.H.), Kasim Khan and Bahadur Kambu brought. . . . 400 Christian prisoners, male and female, young and old, with the idols of their worship, to the presence of the faith-defending Emperor. He ordered that the principles of the Muhammadan religion should be explained to them, and that they should be called upon to adopt it. A few appreciated the honour offered to them and embraced the faith: they experienced the kindness of the Emperor. But the majority in perversity and wilfulness rejected the proposal. These were distributed among the *amirs,* who were directed to keep these despicable wretches in rigorous confinement. When any one of them accepted the true faith, a report was to be made to the Emperor, so that provision might be made for him. Those who refused were to be kept in continual confinement. So it came to pass that many of them passed from prison to hell. Such of their idols as were likenesses of the prophets were thrown into the Jumna, the rest were broken to pieces.

LAST OF THE NIZAM SHAHS

(Text, vol. i. p. 540.) Islam Khan returned to Court, bringing with him the captive Nizam Shah and Fath Khan, whom Khan-khanan Mahabat Khan had sent together with the plunder taken at Daulatabad. Nizam Shah was placed in the custody of Khan-Jahan, in the fort of Gwalior. . . . The crimes of Fath Khan were mercifully pardoned; he was admitted into the Imperial service, and received a *khil'at* and a grant of two *lacs* of rupees per annum. His property also was relinquished to him, but that of Nizam Shah was confiscated.

BADSHAH-NAMA

SEVENTH YEAR OF REIGN, 1043 A.H. (1633 A.D.)

(p. 545.) The Emperor had never visited Lahore, one of his chief cities, since his accession. He now determined to proceed thither, and also to pay a visit to the peerless vale of Kashmir. Accordingly he set out from Agra on the 3rd Sha'ban, 1043 H. . . His Majesty's sense of justice and consideration for his subjects induced him to order that the *Bakhshi* of the *ahadis* with his archers should take charge of one side of the road, and the *Mir-atish* with his matchlock-men should guard the other, so that the growing crops should not be trampled under foot by the followers of the royal train. As, however, damage might be caused, *daroghas*, *mushrifs* and *amins* were appointed to examine and report on the extent of the mischief, so that *raiyats*, and *jagirdars* under 1000, might be compensated for the individual loss they had sustained.

March of Prince Shah Shuja' against Parenda

(Text, vol. ii. p. 33.) The fortress of Parenda, belonging to Nizam Shah, was formerly besieged by 'Azam Khan, but, as before related, certain obstacles compelled him to raise the seige. 'Adil Khan (*by cajolery and bribery*) got the fort into his possession. . . The reduction of this fortress had long been a favourite object with Khan-khanan, and, when Prince Shah Shuja' came near to Burhanpur with a fine army,. . . Khan-khanan, waited upon him, and advised him to undertake the reduction of Parenda. So the Prince, without entering Burhanpur, turned off and marched against that fortress. . . . On arriving at Parenda, he encamped on a stream about a *kos* distant, which is the only water to be found in the vicinity. Then he allotted the work of constructing the trenches, and placed the general direction of the siege works in the hands of Alla Vardi Khan. (*Many conflicts and skirmishes in the neighbourhood.*)

The efforts of the besiegers in the construction of

mines were not attended with much success. The enemy broke into some and destroyed them, and water burst into others. One, constructed by Alla Vardi, in front of the Sher-Haji, was fired by the Prince himself, who went to it by the covered way. It blew up a bastion, but did not make a practicable breach. Moreover, great ill feeling had sprung up between Khan-khanan and Khan-dauran, because the latter was continually repeating that he had saved Khan-khanan's life (*in one of the engagements*). All the nobles and officers also were aggrieved at the petulance and discourtesy of Khan-khanan. Through this the enemy got information about Khan-khanan's plans, and were able to foil them, so that he made no progress in the reduction of the place. He therefore represented to the Prince that, although provisions were abundant, there was no grass or fuel within ten or twelve *kos* of the camp, so that every foraging party had to travel more than twenty *kos*. This was very distressing to the army. The rainy season also was at hand. So he advised a retreat to Burhanpur. As the Prince had been ordered to act upon the advice of Khan-khanan, the army retreated on the 3rd Zi-l hijja.

DEATH OF KHAN-KHANAN

(Text, vol. ii. p. 59.) On the 14th Jumada-l awwal intelligence arrived of the death of Mahabat Khan Khan-khanan, who died of fistula, with which he had long been afflicted.

EIGHTH YEAR OF THE REIGN, 1044 A.H. (1634 A.D.)

The Peacock Throne

(p. 62.) In the course of years many valuable gems had come into the Imperial jewel-house, each one of which might serve as an ear-drop for Venus, or would adorn the girdle of the Sun. Upon the accession of the Emperor, it occurred to his mind that, in the opinion of far-seeing men, the acquisition of such rare jewels and the keeping of such wonderful brilliants can only render one service, that of adorning the throne of empire. They ought therefore, to be put to such a use, that beholders might share in and benefit by their splendour, and that Majesty might shine with increased brilliancy. It was accordingly ordered that, in addition to the jewels in the Imperial jewel-house, rubies, garnets, diamonds, rich pearls and emeralds, to the value of 200 *lacs* of rupees, should be brought for the inspection of the Emperor, and that they, with some exquisite jewels of great weight, exceeding 50,000 *miskals,* and worth eighty-six *lacs* of rupees, having been carefully selected, should be handed over to Be-badal Khan, the superintendent of the gold-smith's department. There was also to be given to him one *lac* of *tolas* of pure gold, equal to 250,000 *miskals* in weight and fourteen *lacs* of rupees in value. The throne was to be three *gaz* in length, two and a half in breadth, and five in height, and was to be set with the above-mentioned jewles. The outside of the canopy was to be of enamel work with occasional gems, the inside was to be thickly set with rubies, garnets, and other jewels, and it was to be supported by twelve emerald columns. On the top of each pillar there were to be two peacocks thick set with gems, and between each two peacocks a tree set with rubies and diamonds, emeralds and pearls. The ascent was to consist of three steps set with jewles of fine water. This throne was completed in the course of seven years at a cost of 100 *lacs* of rupees. Of the eleven jewelled recesses (*takhta*) formed around it for cushions, the middle one, intended for the seat of the Emperor, cost ten *lacs* of rupees. Among the jewels set in this recess was a ruby worth a *lac* of rupees, with Shah 'Abbas, the king of Iran, had presented to the late Emperor Jahangir, who sent it to his present Majesty, the Sahib Kiran-i sani, when he accomplished the conquest of the Dakhin. On it were engraved the names of Sahib-kiran (Timur), Mir Shah Rukh, and Mirza Ulugh Beg. When in course of time it came into the possession of Shah 'Abbas, his name was added; and when Jahangir obtained it, he added the name of himself and of his father.[16] Now it received the addition of the name of his most gracious Majesty Shah Jahan. By command of the Emperor, the following *masnawi*, by Haji Muhammad Jan, the final verse of which contains the date, was placed upon the inside of the canopy in letters of green enamel. . . .

On his return to Agra, the Emperor held a court, sat for the first time on his throne. . . . Yaminu-d daula Asaf Khan was promoted to the dignity of Khan-khanan. *(Conquest by Najabat Khan of several forts belonging to the zamindars of Srinagar, and his subsequent enforced retreat.)*

REBELLION OF JAJHAR SINGH BUNDELA AND HIS SON BIKRAMAJIT

(Text, vol. ii. p. 94) His Majesty in the second year of

[16] *The following is the account given of the throne in the Shah-Jahan-nama of 'Inayat Khan: "The Nau-roz of the year 1044 fell on the 'Id-i fitr, when His Majesty was to take his seat on the new jewelled throne. This gorgeous structure, with a canopy supported on twelve pillars, measured three yards and a half in length, two and a half in breadth, and five in height, from the flight of steps to the overhanging dome. On his Majesty's accession to the throne, he had commanded that eighty-six lacs worth of gems and precious stones, and a diamond worth fourteen lacs, which together make a crore of rupees as money is reckoned in Hindustan, should he used in its decoration. It was completed in seven years, and among the precious stones was a ruby worth a lac of rupees that Shah 'Abbas Safavi had sent to the late Emperor, on which were inscribed the names of the great Timur Sahib-Kiran, etc".*

his reign pardoned the misdeeds of this turbulent man, and sent him on service to the Dakhin. After a while he took leave of Mahabat Khan Khan-khanan, the ruler of the Dakhin, and retired to his own country, leaving behind him son Bikramajit, entitled Jagraj, and his contingent of men. On reaching home, he attacked Bim Narain, Zamindar of Garha, and induced him by a treaty and promise to surrender the fort of Chauragarh.[47] Afterwards, in violation of his engagement, he put Bim Narain and a number of his followers to death, and took possession of the fort, with all the money and valuables it contained. Bim Narain's son accompanied Khandauran to Court from Malwa, taking with him an offering, and he made known to the Emperor what had happened. A *farman* was then sent to Jajhar Singh, charging him with having killed Bim Narain, and taking possession of Garha, wihout the authority of the Emperor, and directing him to surrender the territory to the officers of the Crown, or else to give up the *jagirs* he held in this own country, and to send to Court ten *lacs* of rupees in cash out of the money which had belonged to Bim Narain. He got notice of this *farman* from his *vakils* before it arrived, and being resolved to resist, he directed his son Bikramjit to escape with his troops from the Balaghat, whither he had gone with Khan-dauran, and to make the best of his way home. The son acted accordingly, . . . but he was attacked at Ashta[48] in Malwa by Khan-zaman, *Nazim* of the Payin-ghat, when many of his men were killed, and he himself was wounded, and narrowly escaped; . . . . but he made his way by difficult and unknown roads through the jungles and hills, and joined his father in the *pargana* of Dhamuni.[49] (20,000 *men sent against the rebel*

[47]*Seventy miles W. of Jabalpur.—Ain-i Akbari, vol. i. p.* 367.

[48]*Sixty miles S. W. of Bhopal.*

[49]*In Bundelkhand near lat.* 79°, *long.* 24°.

under the nominal command of Prince Aurangzeb.)

The different divisions of the Imperial army united at Bhander, and prepared for the reduction of the fortress of Undcha. On arriving within three *kos* of Undcha, where the forest territory of Jajhar commences, the forces were constantly occupied in cutting down trees and forming roads. Every day they made a little advance. Jajhar had with him in Undcha nearly 5000 horse and 10,000 foot, and was resolved to contest the passage through the woods. Every day he sent out cavalry and infantry to keep under the cover of the trees, and to annoy the royal forces with muskets and arrows. But the Imperial army killed some of them every day, and forced its way to the neighbourhood of Kahmar-wali, one *kos* from Undcha, where the rebels were determined to fight.

Raja Debi Singh, with the advanced guard of Khan-dauran, pressed forward and took the little hill of Kaḥmar-wali from Jajhar's men. Notwithstanding the density and strength of his forests, Jajhar was alarmed at the advance of the Imperial forces, and removed his family, his cattle and money, from Undcha to the fort of Dhamuni, which his father had built. On the east, north and south of this fort there are deep ravines, which prevent the digging of mines or the running of zigzags. On the west side a deep ditch had been dug twenty imperial yards wide, stretching from ravine to ravine. Leaving a force to garrison Undcha, he himself, with Bikramajit, and all their connexions, went off to Dhamuni. This flight encouraged the royal forces, and on the 2nd Jumada-s sani (*they took Undcha by escalade*), and the garrison fled.

After resting one day at Undcha, the royal army crossed the river Satdhara, on which the town stands, and went in pursuit of the rebels. On the 14th it was three *kos* from Dhamuni, when intelligence came in that

Jajhar had fled with his family and property to the fort of Chauragarh, on the security of which he had great reliance. . . . Before leaving he blew up the buildings round the fort of Dhamuni, and left one of his officers and a body of faithful adherents to garrison the fort. . . . The Imperial army was engaged two days in felling trees and clearing a passage, and then reached the fortress. They pushed their trenches to the edge of the ditch, and pressed the garrison hard. The fort kept up a heavy fire till midnight, when alarmed at the progress of the besiegers, they sent to propose a capitulation. Favoured by the darkness, the men of the garrison made their way out, and hid in the jungles. . . . The Imperial forces then entered the place, and began to sack it. . . . A cry arose that a party of the enemy still held possession of a bastion. . . . 'Ali Asghar and the men under him carried the tower; but while they were engaged in plundering, a spark from a torch fell upon a heap of gunpowder, which blew up the bastion with eighty yards of the wall on both sides, although it was ten yeards thick. 'Ali Asghar and his followers all perished. . .Nearly 300 men and 200 horses who were near the entrance of the fort were killed. . . .

Jajhar, on hearing of the approach of the Imperial forces, destroyed the guns of the fortress (of Chauragarh), burnt all the property he had there, blew up the dwellings which Bim Narain had built within the fort, and then went off with his family and such goods as he could carry to the Dakhin. . . .The Imperial army t' n took possession of the fortress. A *chaudhari* brought in information that Jajhar had with him nearly 2000 horse and 4000 foot. He had also sixty elephants, some of which were loaded with gold and silver money and gold and silver vessels, others carried the members of his family. He travelled at the rate of four Gondi *kos,* that is, nearly eight ordinary *kos* per diem. Although he had got fifteen days' start, the Imperial army set out in pursuit, and for fear the rebel should escape with his family and wealth, the pursures hurried on at the rate of ten Gondi *kos* a day. (*Long and exciting chase.*) When pressed hard by the pursuers, Jajhar and Bikramjit put to death several women whose horses were worn out, and then turned upon their pursuers. . . . Although they fought desperately, they were beaten, and fled into the woods. . . Intelligence afterwards was brought that Jajhar had sent off his family and treasure towards Golkonda, intending to follow them himself. . . . The royal forces consequently steadily pursued their course to Golkonda. . . .

At length the pursuers came in sight of the rebels. Khan-dauran then sent his eldest son, Saiyid Muhammad, and some other officers with 500 horse, to advance with all speed against them. The hot pursuit allowed the rebels no time to perform the rite of *Jauhar,* which is one of the benighted practices of Hindustan. In their despair they inflicted two wounds with a dagger on Rani Parbati. the chief wife of Raja Nar Singh Deo, and having stabbed the other women and children with swords and daggers, they were about to make off. when the pursuers came up and put many of them to the sword. Khan-dauran then arrived, and slew many who were endeavouring to escape. Durgbahan, son of Jajhar, and Durjan Sal, son of Bikramajit, were made prisoners. Udbahan, and his brother Siyam Dawa, sons of Jajhar, who had fled towards Golkonda, were soon afterwards taken. Under the direction of Khan-dauran, Rani Parbati and the other wounded women were raised from the ground and carried to Firoz Jang. The royal army then encamped on the edge of a tank. . . .While they rested there, information was brought that Jajhar and Bikramajit, . . . after escaping from the bloody conflict, had fled to hide themselves in the wilds, where they were killed with great cruelty by the Gonds who inhabit that country. . . .Khan-dauran rode forth to seek their bodies. and having found them, cut off their heads and sent them to Court. . . . When they arrived, the Emperor ordered them to be hung up over the gate of Sehur.

On arriving at Chanda, the Imperial commanders resolved to take tribute from Kipa, chief *zamindar* of Gondwana, . . . and he consented to pay five *lacs* of rupees as tribute to the government, and one *lac* of rupees in cash and goods to the Imperial commanders. . .

On the 13th Jumada-s sani the Emperor proceeded on his journey to Undcha, and on the 21st intelligence arrived of the capture of the fort of Jhansi, one of the strongest in the Bundela country.

NINTH YEAR OF THE REIGN, 1045 A.H. (1635 A.D.)

(Text, vol. i. part 2, p. 125.) An officer was sent to Bijapur to 'Adil Khan, with a *khil'at*, etc., and he was directed to require that 'Adil Khan should be faithful in his allegiance and regular in the payment of his tribute, that he should surrender to the Imperial officers the territories he had taken from Nizamu-l Mulk, and that he should expel the evil-minded Sahu and other adherents of the Nizamu-l Mulk from his dominions. (*Text of the farman.*)

Farman to Kutbu-l Mulk (of Golkonda)

(It stipulates for the allegiance of Kutbu-l Mulk to the imperial throne, for the khutba being read in the name of the Emperor, and for the payment of tribute, etc).

(p. 133.) On the 15th Sha'ban Khan-dauran came from Chanda to wait upon the Emperor. He presented . . . the wives of the wretched Jajhar, Durgbahan his son, and Durjan Sal, his grandson. By the Emperor's order they were made Musalmans by the names of Islam Kuli, and 'Ali Kuli, and they were both placed in the charge of Firoz Khan Nazir. Rani Parbati, being severely wounded, was passed over; the other women were sent to attend upon the ladies of the Imperial palace.

'ABDU-L HAMID LAHORI

DESPATCH OF THE IMPERIAL ARMY AGAINST SAHU AND OTHER NIZAM-SHAHIS

(p. 135.) Nizamu-l Mulk was in confinement in the fort of Gwalior, but the evil-minded Sahu, and other turbulent Nizamu-l Mulkis, had found a boy of the Nizam's family, to whom they gave the title of Nizamu-l Mulk. They had got possession of some of the Nizam's territories, and were acting in opposition to the Imperial government. Now that the Emperor was near Daulatabad, he determined to send Khan-dauran, Khan-zaman, and Shayista Khan, at the head of three different divisions, to punish these rebels, and in the event of 'Adil Khan failing to co-operate with them, they were ordered to attack and ravage his territories. . . . Khan-dauran's force consisted of about 20,000 horse, and he was sent towards Kandahar and Nander, which join the territories of Golkonda and Bijapur, with directions to ravage the country and to besiege the forts of Udgir[50] and Usa, two of the strongest forts in those parts. . . . Khan-zaman's force also consisted of about 20,000 men. He was directed to proceed to Ahmadnagar, and subdue the native territory of Sahu, which lies in Chamar-gonda[51] and Ashti near to Ahmadnagar. After that he was to release the Kokan from the grasp of Sahu, and upon receipt of instructions was to attack and lay waste the country of 'Adil Khan. . . . The force under Shayista Khan consisted of about 8,000 horse, and was sent against the forts of Junir, Sangamnir, Nasik and Trimbak. On the 8th Ramazan they were sent on their respective expeditions. . . . On the 5th Shawal Shayista Khan reported the capture of the fort of Masij.

Udbihan, the son of Jajhar, and his younger

[50]*About fifty miles S. of Nander on the road to Bidar.*

[51]*About fifty miles S. of Ahmadnagar. The "Chambargoondee" of the Bombay Route Map.*

brother, Siyam Dawa,[52] who had fled to Golkonda, were made prisoners by Kutbu-l Mulk, and were sent in custody to the Emperor. They arrived on the 7th Shawwal. The young boy was ordered to be made a Musulman, and to be placed in charge of Firoz Khan *Nazir*, along with the son of Bikramajit. Udbihan and Siyam Dawa, who were of full age, were offered the alternative of Islam or death. They chose the latter, and were sent to hell.

It now became known that 'Adil Khan, misled by evil counsels, and unmindful of his allegiance, had secretly sent money to the commandant of forts Udgir and Usa. He had also sent Khairiyat Khan with a force to protect those two forts, and had commissioned Randaula to support Sahu. Incensed with these acts, the Emperor sent a force of about 10,000 men under Saiyid Khan-Jahan, . . . to chastise him. Orders were given that he and Khan-dauran and Khan-zaman should march into the Bijapur territories in three different directions, to prevent Randaula from joining Sahu, and to ravage the country from end to end. If 'Adil Khan should awake from his heedless stupidity, and should pay proper obedience, they were to hold their hands; if not, they were to make every exertion to crush him. On the 11th a letter arrived from Shayista Khan, reporting that Salih Beg, the Nizamu-l Mulki commander of the fort of Kher-darak, had confined all Sahu's men who were in the fort, and had surrendered it and its dependencies to the Imperial commanders.

Mir Abu-l Hasan and Kazi Abu Sa'id, whom 'Adil Khan of Bijapur had sent to the Emperor after being aroused from his negligence by the despatch of the Imperial forces to ravage his dominions, now arrived and presented tribute and presents.

Mukarramat Khan, the Imperial envoy, approached

[52]*These names are here spelt "Udihan" and "Siyam Duda."*

Bijapur, and 'Adil Khan, fearing the consequences of showing disobedience, came forth from the city five *kos* to meet him, and made great show of submission and respect. . . . But the envoy soon discovered that, although he made all these outward demonstrations through fear, he was really desirous of exciting disturbances and offering opposition. He made a report to this effect, and upon his arrival, the Imperial order was given to kill and ravage as much as possible in the Bijapur territories.

When 'Abdu-l Latif, the envoy to Golkonda, approached the city, Kutbu-l Mulk came forth five *kos* to receive him, and conducted him to the city with great honour. . . . He had the *khutba* read aloud in the name of the Emperor; he several times attended when the *khutba* was read, and bestowed gifts upon the reader, and he had coins struck in the Emperor's name, and sent speciments of them to Court.

(Conquest of the fort of Chandor. Surrender of the hill fort of Anjarai, and of the hill forts of Kanjna and Manjna, Rola, Jola, Ahunat, Kol, Busra, Achlagar, and others. Conquest of the fort of the Raja of Bir after two months' siege. Surrender of the fort of Dharab to Allah Verdi Khan.)

(Shayista Khan takes Sangamnir and the town of Junir from Sahu. Sahu's son attempts the recovery of Junir.)

CAMPAIGN AGAINST BIJAPUR

(Text, vol. i. part 2, p. 151.) On the 8th Shawwal, a royal order reached Khan-dauran near Udgir, informing him that 'Adil Khan had been remiss in his obedience and payment of tribute; that Khan-jahan had been directed to invade his territory by way of Sholapur. Khan-zaman by way of Indapur;[53] and that he, Khan-

[53]*Between Puna and Sholapur, eighty-four miles from the former.*

dauran, must march against him by way of Bidar, and lay waste his country. Khan-dauran accordingly left his baggage on the banks of the Wanjira, in charge of a party of men whose horses were ineffective. In the beginning of New Year's night he set forth, and at five o'clock reached Kalyan, the most flourishing place in that country The inhabitants were quite unprepared, and near 2,000 of them fell under his attack. Many were taken prisoners, and great booty was secured. (*Narainpur, Bhalki, and Maknath,*[54] *taken in succession and plundered. 2,000 of the enemy defeated near Bidar*).

From Bhalki Khan-dauran marched to Deoni, three *kos* from Udgir, and from thence towards Bijapur, plundering and laying waste all the country. He then attacked and sacked the two great towns of Sultanpur and Hirapur. From Hirapur he advanced to the river Bhunra.[55] A party of the enemy then drew near and threatened him, . . . but was defeated. After this, Khan-dauran marched to Firozabad, twelve *kos* from Bijapur. A letter then arrived from Mukarramat Khan, informing him that the Bijapuris had broken down the tank of Shahpur, and had taken all the inhabitants of the country round Bijapur into that city, and that no water or food was to be found in the country. . . . A letter from the Emperor then reached him, to the effect that 'Adil Khan had sent two envoys to make some representations about the forts of Usa and Udgir; but as these belonged to Nizamu-l Mulk, the Emperor would not present them to him. A report received subsequently from Mukarramat Khan stated that 'Adil Khan had

[54]*Narainpur is "one kos and a half from Kalyan." Bhalki or Balki is about equi-distant N. of Kalyan and Bidar. Maknath is "ten kos from Bhalki, and two from Bidar."*

[55]*This name often occurs, and is evidently used for the Bhima.*

abandoned his claim to these forts, and had returned to his obedience. Khan-dauran was therefore directed to desist from ravaging the Bijapur territories, and to lay siege to Usa and Udgir. On the 23rd Muharram Khan-dauran marched against Udgir.

CAMPAIGN OF KHAN-JAHAN

(Text, vol. i. part 2, p. 155.) (*Capture of Saradhun, Dharasiyun, Kanti six kos from Sholapur, and the town of Deoganw. Victories over the Bijapuris, commanded by Randaula.*) Water and provisions were now difficult to obtain, so the royal army fell back to Dharasiyun,[56] intending to leave their baggage at Saradhun, and passing between Usa and Naldrug, to make a raid into the flourshing country about Kulbarga, to plunder and lay waste. On the 1st Zi-l hijja, the enemy made his appearance while the Imperial army was encamped about two *kos* from Usa and began to throw in rockets. The royal forces issued from their entrenchments and repulsed their assailants. Next day they attacked the Imperial army as it was about to march, . . . but were defeated and driven back. After returning from the battle-field, Saiyid Khan-jahan, considering that the country was devastated, and the rains were at hand, determined to fall back to Bir . . . . and await the Imperial directions as to where the rainy season should be passed. On the 11th Zi-l hijja, about eight *kos* from Saradhun, the enemy again appeared in the rear (*and after a hard fight fell back defeated*). The royal army then continued its march to Saradhun, and along the banks of the Wanjira to Dharur.

CAMPAIGN OF KHAN-ZAMAN

(Text, vol. i. part 2, p. 160.) After receiving his orders, Khan-zaman marched to Ahmadnagar, and, after provi-

[56] "*Deraseo,*" *fifty miles north-east of Sholapur.*

sioning his forces, . . . he went on towards Junir. Six *kos* from Ahmadnagar, he learnt that the villain Sahu had made terms with Minaji Bhonsla, and had obtained from him the fort of Mahuli. Having taken Minaji along with him to Junir, Sahu was about to proceed by way of Parganw to Parenda. Khan-zaman marched after him, . . . but Sahu passed the river Bhunra, and proceeded to Lohganw, a dependency of Puna in the Bijapur territories. Here Khan-zaman halted, because his orders were not to follow Sahu into 'Adil Khan's country. (*Capture of the fort of Chamar-gonda by a detachment.*) On receiving orders from Court, he entered the Bijapur territories, and plundered and destroyed every inhabited place he came to. On the 27th Shawwal he reached the pass of Dudbai, where he halted, . . . Next morning he ascended the pass. In eight days he arrived at Kolapur, and invested the fortress and town. Notwithstanding a brave defence, he quickly took the place. (*Successful skirmishes with Sahu and the Bijapuris.*) Khan-zaman next marched to Miraj, one of the principal towns in the Bijapur dominions, and plundered it. From thence he made six days' march to Rai-bagh, a very ancient town in that country, where he obtained great booty. After remaining there ten days, he fell back, and the enemy had the audacity to hang upon his rear and harass him with rockets. Eight days' march from Miraj the army encamped on the bank of a river. A party sent out to forage, and a force was ordered to support it. The enemy attacked this force, and a sharp fight ensued; but the assailants were repulsed and pursued for two *kos*. While the army was resting on the banks of the river Bhunra, an Imperial farman arrived, directing Khan-zaman to return to the royal presence, to receive instructions for the reduction of the fort of Junir and the punishment of Sahu. The reason for this was that 'Adil Khan had submitted, had agreed to pay a tribute equivalent to twenty *lacs* in jewels, elephants, etc., and engaged that if Sahu returned and surrendered Junir and the other forts in the Nizam-Shahi territory to the imperial officers, he would take him into his service; but if Sahu did not do so, he would assist the Imperial forces in reducing the forts and punishing Sahu.

(*Capture by Khan-khanan of the forts of Anki and Tanki, Alka and Palka, eighteen kos from Daulatabad.*)

(*Farman containing the terms of peace with 'Adil Khan, and letter of the latter in acknowledgment. Latter of homage from Kutbu-l Mulk. Summary of Shah Jahan's two expeditions to the Dakhin, the first in his father's lifetime, the second after his own accession.*)

'ADIL KHAN OF BIJAPUR

(Text, vol. i. part 2, p. 202.) While the Emperor was still thinking about the reduction of the forts of the Dakhin, 'Adil Khan, being disturbed by the prolonged stay of the Imperial Court, wrote a letter to the Emperor, representing that the affairs of that country were now all settled, and that he would be answerable for the surrender of the forts held by Sahu and others. There was therefore no reason for the Emperor's staying any longer and it would be a great favour if he would proceed to the capital, so that the *raiyats* and people of Bijapur might return peacefully to their avocations. The Emperor graciously consented, and resolved to go and spend the rainy season at Mandu. 'Adil Khan's tribute, consisting of . . . , arrived, and was accepted. The Emperor confirmed to him the territory of Bijapur and the fortress of Parenda, which had formerly belonged to Nizamu-l Mulk, but which the commandant had surrendered to 'Adil Khan for a bribe. He also confirmed to him all the country of Kokan on the sea-shore, which had been formerly held half by him and half by Nizamu-l Mulk. (*Copy of the*

BADSHAH-NAMA

PRINCE AURANGZEB, GOVERNOR OF THE DAKHIN

(Text, vol. i, part 2, p. 205.) On the 3rd Zi-l hijja the Emperor appointed Prince Aurangzeb to the government of the Dakhin. This country contains sixty-four forts, fifty-three of which are situated on hills, the remaining eleven are in the plain. It is divided into four *subas*. 1. Daulatabad, with Ahmadnagar and other districts, which they call the *suba* of the Dakhin. The capital of this province, which belonged to Nizamu-l Mulk, was formerly Ahmadnagar, and afterwards Daulatabad. 2. Telingana. This is situated in the *suba* of the Balaghat.[57] 3. Khandes. The fortress of this province is Asir, and the capital is Burhanpur, situated four *kos* from Asir. 4. Birar. The capital of this province is Elichpur, and its famous fortress is called Gawli. It is built on the top of a hill, and is noted above all the fortress in that country for strength and security. The whole of the third province and a part of the fourth is in the Payin-ghat. The *jama'*, or total revenue of the four provinces is two *arbs* of *dams*, equivalent to five crores of rupees.

(*Treaty with Kutbu-l Mulk. Letter from the latter.*)

(*Khan-dauran besieges Udgir and Usa, and both forts are eventually surrendered.*)

TENTH YEAR OF THE REIGN, 1046 A.H. (1636 A.D.)

Conquest of the Fort of Junir and Settlement of the Dakhin

(Text, vol. i. part 2. p. 225.) When Khan-zaman returned from the Emperor to his army, he learnt that Sahu had declined entering into the service of 'Adil Khan, and refused to surrender Junir and the other fortresses to the Imperial officers. 'Adil Khan therefore sent his forces, under the command of Randaula, to co-operate

[57] *The Shah-Jahan-nama adds, "The capital of which is called Nander and the fortress Kandahar."*

with the Imperial army in the destruction of Sahu, and the reduction of his fortresses. Khan-zaman hastened to Junir, . . . and invested the fortress. Being satisfied with the arrangements for the siege, he determined to march against Sahu, who was in the neighbourhood of Puna. When he reached the Khorandi, he was detained on its banks for a month by the heavy rains and the inundations. As soon as the waters abated, he crossed the river, and encamped on the banks of the Indan, near Lohganw, and Sahu, who was seventeen *kos* distant, then made into the mountains of Gondhana and Nurand. There were three large swollen rivers, the Indan, the Mol, and the Mota,[58] between Khan-zaman and Sahu. . . . The Khan therefore sent an officer to consult with Randaula. The opinion of that commander coincided with Khan-zaman's in favour of the pursuit, and the latter began his march. . . . Sahu then fled with great haste by the pass of Kombha,[59] and entered the Kokan. . . . Finding no support there, he returned by the pass of Kombha. The Imperial forces then entered the Kokan by the same pass, and Randaula also was closing up. Sahu then went off to Mahuli, . . . and from thence to the fort of Muranjan,[60] situated between the hills and the jungle. Khan-zaman followed. . . . On discovering the approach of his pursuers, Sahu hastily sent off a portion of his baggage, and abandoned the rest. . . . The pursuers having come up, put many of the rebels to the sword. . . . Being still pursued, Sahu went again to Mahuli, hoping to get away by Trimbak and Tringalwari;[61] but, fearing lest he should encounter the royal forces, he halted at

[58]*The Indiranee, Moola, and Moota of the Maps, near Puna.*

[59]*In the Ghats, Lat.* 18·20.

[60]*Or "Muroranjan" in the Ghats, Lat.* 18·50.

[61]*A little N. of the Tal Ghat.*

Mahuli. He retained a party of his adherents, who had long followed him, and the rest of his men he disbanded, and allowed them to go where they would. Then, with his son and a portion of his baggage, he went into the fort, resolved to stand a siege.

Khan-zaman got intelligence of this when he was twelve *kos* from Mahuli, and, notwithstanding the difficulties of the road, he reached the fort in one day. . . . He immediately opened his trenches and made approaches. . . . A few days after Randaula came up, and joined in the siege. . . . When the place was hard pressed, Sahu wrote repeatedly to Khan-zaman, offering to surrender the fortress on condition of being received into the Imperial service. He was informed that if he wished to save his life, he must come to terms with 'Adil Khan, for such was the Emperor's command. He was also advised to be quick in doing so, if he wished to escape from the swords of the besiegers. So he was compelled to make his submission to 'Adil Khan, and he besought that a treaty might be made with him. After the arrival of the treaty, he made some absurd inadmissible demands, and withdrew from the agreement he had made. But the siege was pressed on, and the final attack drew near, when Sahu came out of the fort and met Randaula half way down the hill, and surrendered himself with the young Nizam. He agreed to enter the service of 'Adil Khan, and to surrender the fortress of Junir and the other forts to the Imperial generals. . . . Accordingly the forts of Junir, Trimbak, Tringalwari, Haris, Judhan, Jund, and Harsira, were delivered over to Khan-zaman. . . . Randaula, under the orders of 'Adil Khan, placed the young Nizam in the hands of Khan-zaman, and then went to Bijapur. accompanied by Sahu.

(Khan-dauran takes possession of the forts of Kataljhar, and Ashta, and besieges and storms the fort of Nagpur.)

NIZAMU-L MULK

(Text. vol. i. part 2, 256.) On the 1st Zi-l hijja, 1046 A.H. Prince Murad Bakhsh, Yaminu-d daula Khan-dauran Bahadur Nusrat Jang,[62] and others went forth to meet Prince Aurangzeb, who had returned to Court from the Dakhin. . . . He brought with him the member of Nizamu-l Mulk's family[63] whom the disaffected of the Dakhin had made use of for their rebellious purposes, and to whom they had given the title of Nizamu-l Mulk. He was placed under the charge of Saiyid Khan-Jahan, to be kept in the fort of Gwalior, where there were two other of the Nizams—one of whom was made prisoner at the capture of Ahmadnagar in the reign of Jahangir, and the other at the downfall of Daulatabad in the present reign. . . . On the 4th, the news came that Khan-zaman had died at Daulatabad from a complication of diseases of long standing. . . . Shayista Khan was appointed to succeed him in his command.

THE BUNDELAS

(Text. vol. i. part 2, p. 270). The Bundelas are a turbulent troublesome race. Notwithstanding that Jajhar, their chief, had been slain, the rebellious spirits of the tribe had taken no warning, but had set up a child of his named Pirthi Raj, who had been carried off alive from the field of battle, and they had again broken out in rebellion. . . . Khan-dauran Bahadur Nusrat Jang was ordered to suppress this insurrection, and then to proceed to his government in Malwa.

STORM AT THATTA

(p. 276.) On the 23rd Rabi'u-l awwal letters were

[62] *He had been honoured with this title for his late victories.*

[63] *This individual, like all the others, is sarcastically called "Be-Nizam."*

BADSHAH-NAMA

received from Thatta, reporting that rain had fallen incessantly for thirty-six hours in all the towns and places near the sea-shore. Many houses and buildings were destroyed, and great numbers of men and beasts of all kinds were drowned. The wind blew so furiously that huge trees were torn up by their roots, and the waves of the sea cast numbers of fishes on to the shore. Nearly a thousand ships, laden and unladen, went down from the violence of the sea, and heavy losses fell upon the ship-owners. The land also, over which the waves were driven, became impregnated with salt, and unfit for cultivation.

CONQUEST OF TIBET

(Text, vol. i. part 2. p. 281.) The late Emperor Jahangir long entertained the design of conquering Tibet, and in the course of his reign Hashim Khan, son of Kasim Khan *Mir-bahr,* governor of Kashmir, under the orders of the Emperor, invaded the country with a large force of horse and foot and local *zamindars.* But although he entered the country, and did his best, he met with no success, and was obliged to retreat with great loss and with much difficulty. . . . The Imperial order was now given that Zafar Khan, governor of Kashmir, should assemble the forces under his command, and effect the conquest of that country. Accordingly he collected nearly eight thousand horse and foot, composed of Imperial forces, men of his own, and retainers of the *marzbans* of his province. He marched by the difficult route of Karcha-barh, and in the course of one month he reached the district of Shkardu, the first place of importance in Tibet, and on this side of the Nilab (Indus). 'Ali Rai, father of Abdal, the present *Marzban* of Tibet, had built upon the summits of two high mountains two strong forts—the higher of which was called Kahar-phucha, and the other Kahchana. Each of them had a road of access "like the neck of a reed, and the curve of a talon." The road of communication between the two was on the top of the mountain. Abdal shut himself up in the fort of Kaharphucha. He placed his minister and general manager in the fort of Kahchana, and he sent his family and property to the fort of Shakar, which stands upon a high mountain on the other side of the Nilab.

Zafar Khan, after examining the height and strength of the fortresses, was of opinion that it was inexpedient to invest and attack them; but he saw that the military and the peasantry of Tibet were much distressed by the harsh rule of Abdal, and he resolved to win them over by kindness. Then he sent a detachment to subdue the fort of Shakar, and to make prisoners of the family of Abdal. The whole time which the army could keep the field in this country was two months; for if it remained longer, it would be snowed up. It was for this reason that he sent Mir Fakhru-d din, . . . with four thousand men, against the fort of Shakar, while he himself watched the fort in which Abdal was. He next sent Hasan, nephew of Abdal, with some other men of Tibet, who had entered into the Imperial service, and some *zamindars* of Kashmir, who had friendly relations with the people of the country, to endeavour by persuasion and promises to gain over the people. . . . Mir Fakhr passed over the river Nilab, and laid siege to the fort. Daulat, son of Abdal, of about fifteen years of age, was in charge of the fort. He sallied out to attack the besiegers, . . . but was driven back with loss. . . . The besiegers then advanced, and opened their trenches against the gate on the Shkardu side. The son of Abdal was so frightened by these proceedings, that, regardless of his father's family (in the fort), he packed up the gold, silver, and what was portable, and escaped in the night by the Kashghar gate. Mir Fakhru-d din, being apprised of his flight, entered the fort. He could not restrain his followers from plundering; but he took charge of Abdal's family. A force was sent in pursuit of the son, which could not overtake him, but returned with some gold and silver he had thrown away on the road.

On hearing of this victory, Zafar Khan pressed on the siege of Kaharphucha and Kahchana. . . . The governor and garrison of the latter surrendered. . . . Abdal, in despair at the progress made by the invadors, and at the loss of his wives and children, opened negotiations and surrendered the fort of Kaharphucha. . . . Zafar Khan was apprehensive that the snow would fall and close the passes, and that, at the instigation of Abdal, he might be attacked from the side of Kashmir. So, without making any settlement of the country, and without searching after Abdal's property, he set out on his return, taking with him Abdal, his family, and some of the leading men of the enemy. He left Muhammad Murad, Abdal's *vakil,* in charge of the country.

ELEVENTH YEAR OF THE REIGN, 1047 A.H. (1637 A.D.)

Capture of Kandahar and other forts[64]

(Text, vol. ii. p. 24.) The strong fortress of Kandahar was annexed to the Imperial dominions in the fortieth year of the Emperor Akbar. . . . Shah Safi of Persia, was desirous of recovering it. In the fifteenth year of the reign of Jahangir, Prince Shah Jahan was sent to arrange the affairs of the Dakhin, . . . and the Shah of Persia seized the opportunity to make an attempt to recover the place. He invested it and after a siege of forty-five days reduced the fortress in the seventeenth year of Jahangir. . . . After a time, 'Ali Mardan Khan was appointed governor of Kandahar, . . . and Shah Jahan, being desirous of recovering the place, directed his governor of Kabul to send an able emissary to 'Ali Mardan Khan, who was to learn what he could about

[64] *The account of this siege is told in great detail.*

the fortress and its garrison, and to make overtures to 'Ali Mardan Khan. . . . The envoy was received very graciously, . . . and friendly relations were established between 'Ali Mardan Khan and the governor of Kabul, . . . so that the Khan at length wrote, expressing his desire to surrender the place to Shah Jahan. . . . On the approach of the Imperial forces, 'Ali Mardan Khan conducted them into the fortress, and gave it up to them. . . . The governor of Kabul was directed to proceed to Kandahar, and to present a *lac* of rupees to 'Ali Mardan Khan. He was then to take the Khan to Kabul, and to send him under escort to the Imperial Court, with all his family and dependents. . . . The Emperor sent 'Ali Mardan Khan a *khil'at* (*and many other fine presents. Engagement between Sa'id Khan, governor of Kabul, and the Persians, and defeat of the latter. Capture by siege of the forts of Bust, Zamind-awar, and Girishk.*) All the country of Kandahar with its fortresses (*enumerated in detail*) were re-annexed to the Imperial dominions.

REBELLION IN KUCH-HAJU

(Text, vol. ii. p. 64.) On the north of the country of Bengal there are two countries: Kuch-Haju, a cultivated country, which lies on the banks of the Brahmaputra, a large river, two *kos* in width, which flows from the country of Asham (Assam) into Bengal. From thence to Jahangir-nagar (Dacca) is one month's journey. The other country is Kuch-Bihar, which is far away from the river, and is twenty days' journey from Jahangir-nagar. These two countries belonged to local rulers (*marzban*), and at the beginning of the reign of the Emperor Jahangir, the country of Kuch-Haju was under the rule of Parichhit, and Kuch-Bihar under Lachhmi Narain, brother of the grandfather of Parichhit. In the eighth year of the reign, Shah Jahan gave the government of Bengal to Shaikh 'Alau-d din Fathpuri, who had received the title of Islam Khan. Raghunath, Zamindar of Susang, came to him, complaining that Parichhit had tyrannically and violently placed his wives and children in prison. His allegations appeared to be true. At the same time, Lachhmi Narain repeatedly represented his devotion to the Imperial government, and incited Islam Khan to effect the conquest of Kuch-Haju. He accordingly sent a force to punish Parichhit, and to subjugate the country. (*Long details of the operations.*) When the victorious army reached the river Kajli, some men were sent over first in boats, who in a short time defeated and put to flight the guard of the place. The whole force then crossed and destroyed some old forts. A strong fort was then constructed on each side of the Kajli, and . . . . garrisons were placed in them to check and keep down the turbulent landholders. The army then proceeded to Koh-hatah, towards Utarkol, between Sri-ghat and the Kajli, there to pass the rains.

CONQUEST OF BAGLANA

(Text, vol. ii. p. 105.) The territory of Baglana contains nine forts, thirty-four *parganas,* and one thousand and one villages. It has been a separate jurisdiction (*marzbani*) for one thousand four hundred years, and it's present ruler is named Bharji. It is famous for its temperate climate, its numerous streams and the abundance of of its trees and fruits. In length it is a hundred *kos,* and in breadth eighty. On the east is Chandor, a dependency of Daulatabad; on the west the port of Surat and the sea; on the north Sultanpur and Namdurbar; and on the south Nasik and Trimbak . . . The strongest of its forts are Salhir and Mulhir.[55] Salhir is placed upon a hill . . . Mulhir also stands upon a hill. . . . When Prince

[55]*"Mooleer" lies about half way, a little west, of a line drawn from Chandor to Nandurbar.*

Aurangzeb was sent to the government of the Dakhin, he was directed to subjugate this country. On the 8th Sha'ban, 1047 H. (Dec. 1637), he sent an army against it, . . . which advanced and laid siege to Mulhir. The trenches were opened and the garrison was pressed so hard that, on the 10 Shawwal, Bharji sent out his mother and his *vakil* with the keys of his eight forts, offering to enrol himself among the servants of the Imperial throne, on condition of receiving the *pargana* of Sultanpur. . . . When this proposal reached the Emperor, he granted Bharji a *mansab* of three thousand personal and 2500 horse, and Sultanpur was conferred upon him for his home.

TWELFTH YEAR OF THE REIGN, 1048 A.H. (1638 A.D.)

(*Submission of Manik Rai, the Mag Raja of Chatgam.*)

(Text, vol. ii. p. 123.) On the 13th Rajab, the Imperial train reached Lahore, . . and 'Ali Mardan Khan, who had come from Kandahar, was received with great ceremony. He was presented with (*numerous rich gifts*), and his *mansab* was increased from 5,000 to 6,000 personal and 6,000 horse. . . . Before the end of the month he was appointed governor of Kashmir, . . and shortly afterwards he was presented with five *lacs* of rupees and ten parcels of the choice fabrics of the looms of Bengal. The Emperor afterwards did him the honour of paying him a visit at his house. (*The Imperial progress from Lahore to Kabul and back again.*)

LITTLE TIBET

(Text, vol. ii. p. 159). The conquest of Little Tibet, the captivity of its ruler Abdal, and the appointment of Adam Khan to be governor, have been previously mentioned. Adam Khan now wrote to 'Ali Mardan Khan, the new governor of Kashmir, informing him that Sangi Bamkhal, the holder of Great Tibet, . . . had seized upon Burag in Little Tibet, and meditated further aggression.

'Ali Mardan Khan sent a force against him under the command of Husain Beg. . . On the meeting of the two forces, Sangi's men were put to flight. . . He then sued for forgiveness, and offered to pay tribute.

THIRTEENTH YEAR OF THE REIGN, 1049 A.H. (1639 A.D.)

On the 21st Jumada-s sani, the Emperor arrived at Lahore. . . 'Ali Mardan Khan came down from Kashmir. . . . His *mansab* was increased to 7,000 personal and 7,000 horse, . . . and the government of the Panjab was given to him in addition to that of Kashmir. . . . On the 6th Rajab, Islam Khan came according to summons from Bengal, and was appointed to the office of Financial Minister (*diwani-kull*).

'ALI MARDAN'S LAHORE CANAL

'Ali Mardan Khan represented to His Majesty that one of his followers was an adept in the forming of canals, and would undertake to construct a canal from the place where the river Ravi descends from the hills into the plains, and to conduct the waters to Lahore, benefiting the cultivation of the country through which it should pass. The Emperor . . gave to the Khan one *lac* of rupees, a sum at which experts estimated the expense, and the Khan then entrusted its formation to one of his trusted servants.

(*Advance of an army from Sistan against Kandahar.—Occupation and abandonment of the fort of Khanshi, near Bust.*)

(*Great fire at the residence of Prince Shuja' in Agra—Royal visit to Kashmir.*)

In the month of Muharram intelligence came in that Pirthi Raj, son of Jajhar Bundela, had been taken prisoner. . . Orders were given for his confinement in the fort of Gwalior.

'ABDU-L HAMID LAHORI

FOURTEENTH YEAR OF THE REIGN, 1050, A.H. (1640 A.D.)

(Chastisement of the Kolis and Kathis in Gujarat.—Payment of tribute by the Jam of Kathiwar.)

(Rebellion of Jagat Singh, son of Raja Basu of Kangra.)

FIFTEENTH YEAR OF THE REIGN, 1051, A.H. (1641 A.D.)

Death of Asaf Khan Khan-khanan

(Text, vol. ii. p. 257.) On the 17th Sha'ban Yaminu-d daula Asaf Khan Khan-khanan, commander-in-chief, departed this life; . . and on receiving the intelligence, His Majesty was much affected, and gave orders that he should be buried on the west side of the tomb of the late Emperor Jahangir, and that a lofty dome should be raised over his grave. . . . He had risen to a rank and dignity which no servant of the State had ever before attained. By the munificent favour of the Emperor, his *mansab* was nine thousand personal and nine thousand horse, *do-aspah* and *sih-aspah,* the pay of which amounted to sixteen *krors* and twenty *lacs* of *dams.* When these had all received their pay, a sum of fifty *lacs* of rupees was left for himself. . . . Besides the mansion which he had built in Lahore, and on which he expended twenty *lacs* of rupees, he left money and valuables to the amount of two *krors* and fifty *lacs* of rupees. There were 30 *lacs* of rupees in jewels, three *lacs* of *ashrafis* equal to 42 *lacs* of rupees, one *kror* and 25 *lacs* in rupees, 30 *lacs* in gold and silver utensils, and 23 *lacs* in miscellaneous articles.

(Campaign in Jagat Singh's territory. Capture of Mu, Nurpur, and other forts. Surrender of Taragarh, and submission of Jagat Singh.)

SIXTEENTH YEAR OF THE REIGN, 1052 A.H. (1642 A.D.)

SEVENTEENTH YEAR OF THE REIGN, 1053 A.H. (1643 A.D.)

(Reduction of Palamun, and submission of its Raja.)

(Text, vol. ii. p. 376.) At the beginning of Rabi'u-s

sani, it was made known to the Emperor that Prince Aurangzeb, under the influence of ill-advised, short-sighted companions, had determined to withdraw from wordly occupations, and to pass his days in retirement. His Majesty disapproved of this, and took from the Prince his *mansab* and his *jagir*, and dismissed him from the office of Governor-General of the Dakhin. Khan-dauran Bahadur Nusrat Jang was appointed to succed him.

EIGHTEENTH YEAR OF THE REIGN, 1054 A.H. (1644 A.D.)

('Ali Murdan Khan Amiru-l Umara sent to chastise Tardi 'Ali Katghan of Balkh.—Successful result.)

(p. 385.) On the 29th Zi-l hijja, Prince Aurangzeb was appointed Governor of Gujarat. . .

NINETEENTH YEAR OF THE REIGN, 1055 A.H. (1645 A.D.)

(Affairs of Nazar Muhammad Khan of Balkh—Operations in Kabul.)

(p. 411.) On the 29th Shawwal, 1055, died Nur Jahan Begam, widow of the late Emperor Jahangir. After her marriage with the Emperor, she obtained such an ascendency over him, and exercised such absolute control over civil and revenue matters, that it would be unseemly to dilate upon it here. After the accession of the Emperor Shah Jahan, he settled an annual allowance of two lacs of rupees upon her.[66]

CAMPAIGN AGAINST BALKH AND BADAKHSHAN

(Text, vol. ii. p. 482.) Ever since the beginning of his reign, the Emperor's heart had been set upon the conquest of Balkh and Badakhshan, which were hereditary

[66] *Khafi Khan says that after Jahangir's death she wore only white clothes, she never went to parties of amusement of her own accord, but lived in private and in sorrow. She was buried at Lahore in a tomb she had built for herself by the side of Jahangir.*

territories of his house, and were the keys to the acquisition of Samarkand, the home and capital of his great ancestor Timur Sahib-Kiran. He was more especially intent on this because Nazar Muhammad Khan had had the presumption to attack Kabul, from whence he had been driven back in disgrace. The prosecution of the Emperor's cherished enterprise had been hitherto prevented by various obstacles; . . but now the foundations of the authority of Nazir Muhammad were shaken, and his authority in Balkh was precarious. . . So the Emperor determined to send his son Murad Bakhsh with fifty thousand horse, and ten thousand musketeers, rocket-men and gunners, to effect the conquest of that country. . . On the last day of Zi-l hijja, 1055 H., the Emperor gave his farewell to Prince Murad Bakhsh, to Amiru-l Umara ('Ali Mardan Khan)[67] and the other officers sent on this service. (*Plan of campaign. . . Progress of the Emperor to Kabul—Details of the campaign.—Capture of the fort of Kahmard and the stronghold of Ghori—Conquest of Kundaz and Balkh, and flight of Nazar Muhammad.—Revenues of Nazar Muhammad.*)

TWENTIETH YEAR OF THE REIGN, 1056 A.H. (1646 A.D.)

(*Prince Murad Bakhsh desires to retire from Balkh.—Displeasure of the Emperor expressed in a despatch.—The Prince persists*). Many of the *amirs* and *mansabdars* who were with the prince concurred in this unreasonable desire. Natural love of home, a preference for the people and the manners of Balkh, and the rigours of the climate, all conduced to this desire. This resolution became a cause of distress among the *raiyats*, of despondency among the soldiery, and of hesitation among the men who were coming into Balkh from all quarters. The soldiers, seeing this vacillation, began to plunder and oppress the people. So, when the Prince's desire was

[67] *Who was of course the real commander.*

repeatedly expressed, the Emperor's anger was increased. He deprived the prince of his *mansab,* and took from him his *tuyul* of Multan. Under these circumstances, to settle the confusion in Balkh, the Emperor found it necessary to send there a trustworthy and able manager; so he selected Sa'du-lla Khan, his Prime Minister. (*Fighting in Badakhshan.—Settlement of Balkh.*) Sa-du-lla Khan returned on the 5th Sha'ban, 1056 H., having settled the affairs of Balkh, and restored order and tranquillity among the soldiers and people, and rescued the country from wretchedness. He had most effectually carried out the orders of the Emperor, and was rewarded with a *khil'at,* and a thousand increase to his *mansab.* (*Prince Murad Bakhsh restored to his mansab of* 12,000.—*Much fighting near Balkh and Shaburghan.*)

AURANGZEB SENT TO BALKH

(Text, vol. ii. p. 627.) On the 24th Zi-l hijja, 1056, the Emperor bestowed the countries of Balkh and Badakhshan on Aurangzeb, and increased his *mansab* to 15,000 personal and ten thousand horse, eight thousand being *do-aspahs* or *sih-aspahs* . . . He was directed to proceed to Peshawar, and on the arrival of spring to march to Balkh, in company with Amiru-l Umara 'Ali Mardan Khan, and a body of Rajputs, who had left Balkh and Badakhshan in disgust, and had come to Peshawar, where they were stopped by an Imperial order directing the officers at Atak not to allow them to cross the Indus.

THE EMPEROR PROCEEDS TO KABUL

(Text, vol. ii. p. 637.) By the reports of the commanders in Balkh and Badakhshan, the Emperor was informed that 'Abdu-l 'Aziz Khan, governor of Turan, . . . intended to invade Balkh at the beginning of spring. On the 15th Muharram Prince Aurangzeb was sent on to Balkh with a body of Imperial soldiers, and the Emperor himself determined to leave Lahore and go to Kabul for the third time.

(Long details of fighting in Balkh and Badakhshan, ending abruptly with a statement of the errors made on the Imperial side.)

SHAHJAHAN-NAMA
OF
'INAYYAT KHA'N

(Muhammad Tahir, who received the title of 'Inayat Khan, and was poetically named 'Ashna, was son of Zafar Khan bin Khwaja Abu-l Hasan.

Zafar Khan, the author's father, was *wazir* of Jahangir. In the reign of Shah Jahan, he was at one time ruler of Kabul, and afterwards of Kashmir, during which latter government he effected the conquest of Tibet recorded in the foregoing pages. At a later period he was appointed to the administration of Thatta. "He was celebrated as a poet, as a patron of letters, and as a just and moderate ruler."

'Inayat Khan's maternal grandfather, Saif Khan, was governor of Agra, and when Prince Shuja' was appointed ruler of Bengal, Saif Khan was sent thither to conduct the administration until the arrival of the prince.

The author, it appears, was born in the year that Shah Jahan came to the throne. In the seventh year of his age he received, as he informs us, "a suitable *mansab.*" He was sent to join his father in Kashmir while he was governor there. He was afterwards *darogha-i dagh,* and subsequently employed in a more congenial office in the Imperial Library. "He inherited his father's talents and good qualities, and is said even to have surpassed him in ability. He was witty and of agreeable manners, and was one of the intimate friends of Shah Jahan. Latterly he retired from office, and settled in Kashmir, where he died in A.H. 1077 (A.D. 1666). In addition to the history of Shah Jahan's reign, he was author of a *Diwan* and three *Masnawis.*"[1]

[1]*Morley's Catalogue.*

'INAYYAT KHAN

The sources of the first part of this *Shah Jahan-nama* are plainly acknowledged by the author. The first twenty years are in entire agreement with the *Badshah-nama*, but are written in a more simple style. The history comes down to 1068 A.H., (1657-8 A.D.), the year in which Aurangzeb was declared Emperor, but of this event he takes no notice. The author does not inform us whether he used any other work after the *Badshah-nama* as the basis of his own, or whether the history of the last ten years is his own independent work.

The following is the author's own account of his work translated from his Preface:

"The writer of these wretched lines, Muhammad Tahir, commonly known as Ashna, but bearing the title of 'Inayat Khan bin Muzaffar Khan bin Khwaja Abu-l Hasan, represents to the attention of men of intelligence, and acumen that in Rabi'u-l awwal, in the 31st year of the reign of the Emperor Shah Jahan (*six lines of titles and phrases*), corresponding to 1068 H., he was appointed superintendent of the Royal Library, and there he found three series of the *Badshah-nama*, written by Shaikh 'Abdu-l Hamid Lahori and others, each series of which comprised the history of ten years of the illustrious reign. The whole of these memoirs completed one *karn*, which is an expression signifying thirty years. Memoirs of the remaining four years were written after his death by others. The author desires to observe that the style of these volumes seemed difficult and diffuse to his simple mind, and so he reflected that, although Shaikh Abu-l Fazl was ordered by the Emperor Akbar to write the history of his reign, yet Khwaja Nizamu-d din Ahmad Bakhshi wrote a distinct history of that reign, which he called the *Tabakat-i Akbar-shahi*. Jannat-makani Nuru-d din Muhammad Jahangir, imitating the example of his ancestor the Emperor Zahiru-d din Muhammad Babar, himself wrote a history of his own reign; yet Mu'tamad Khan Bakhshi wrote a history of that reign, to which he gave the title of *Ikbal-nama-i Jahangiri*. Ghairat Khan Nakshabandi also brought together the chief events of that reign in a book which he called *Ma-asir-i Jahangiri*. (With these examples before him), it seemed to the writer of these pages that, as he and his ancestors had been devoted servants of the Imperial dynasty, it would be well for him to write the history of the reign of Shah Jahan in a simple and clear style, and to reproduce the contents of the three volumes of Shaikh 'Abdu-l Hamid in plain language and in a condensed form. Such a work (he thought) would not be superfluous, but rather a gain. So he set about his work, and the Almighty gave him leisure, so that in a short time he completed it. The history from the fourth to the tenth year is based on the *Padshah-nama* of Muhammad Amin Kazwini, commonly known as Aminai Munshi, which is written in a more simple style. And as only a selection has been made of the events recorded, this work is styled *Mulakhkhas*."

The title *Mulakhkhas* "Abridgment," which the author gave to his work, was too indefinite to last, and it is commonly known as *Shah Jahan-nama*.

MSS. of this work seem to be common. Sir H. M. Elliot has three borrowed copies. There are three in the British Museum, and one in the Library of the Asiatic Society. A copy belonging to the Raja of Benares is a handsome quarto of 12 inches × 8½, and contains 360 leaves of 19 lines to the page. The whole of this work, from the beginning of the third year of the reign to the accession of Aurangzeb, with which it closes, was translated by the late Major Fuller. It fills 561 folio pages of close writing, and is in Sir H. M. Elliot's Library. The following Extracts are taken from that translation.)

EXTRACTS

TWENTY-FIRST YEAR OF THE REIGN, 1057 A.H. (1647 A.D.)

In the news from Balkh, which reached the ear of

royalty about this time, through the representations of the victorious Prince Muhammad Aurangzeb Bahadur, was the following:—Nazar Muhammad Khan, who, after abandoning the siege of fort Maimanah, had stood fast at Nilchiragh,[2] continued watching, both day and night, the efforts of 'Abdul-l 'Aziz Khan and his other sons, who were gone to oppose the royal army with all the Uzbek forces of Mawarau-n Nahr, Balkh and Badakhshan, anxious to see what would be the result. As soon as he heard that they also had, like himself, become wanderers in the desert of failure owing to the superior prowess and vigour of the royalists, finding his hopes everywhere shattered, he despatched an apologizing letter to the illustrious Prince, expressive of his contrition for past misdeeds, and ardent longing for an interview with His Royal Highness, stating that he was desirous of retrieving his fallen fortunes, through the intercessions of that ornament of the throne of royalty. The illustrious Prince having kept the envoy in attendance till the receipt of an answer, waited in expectation of the *farman's* arrival, and the Khan's letter, which His Royal Highness had forwarded to Court in the original, with some remarks of his own, was duly submitted to the auspicious perusal. As it happened, from the commencement of his invasion of Balkh, this very design had been buried in the depths of his comprehensive mind, *viz.* that after clearing the kingdoms of Balkh and Badakhshan from the thorny briers of turbulence and anarchy, he would restore them in safety to Nazar Muhammad Khan. The latter. however, scorning the dictates of prudence, hastened to Iran; but finding his affairs did not progress there to his satisfaction, he turned back, and at the suggestion of the Kalmaks and other associates, came and besieged the fort of Maimanah in order that he might seek shelter within its walls, and so set his mind at rest.

[2]*(Also written Pulchiragh or Bilchiragh.)*

In the end, however, after infinite toil and labour, seeing the capture of the stronghold in question to be beyond his reach, he departed without effecting his object, and moved to Nilchiragh, all which occurrences have been already fully detailed in their proper place. From the letters of reporters in those dominions, it was further made known to his world-adorning understanding, that notwithstanding the servants of the crown had manifested the most laudable zeal and anxiety to console the hearts of the peasantry in Balkh and Badakhshan by giving them seed, and assisting them to plough and till their fields: yet, owing to the inroads of the Almans, most of the grain and crops had been destroyed, and the populous places desolated; and that the commanders of the army, and the chiefs of the soldiery, owing to the dearth of provisions and the scarcity of grain, were extremely disgusted, and averse to remaining any longer in the country. From the contents of the Prince's letter, moreover, his unwillingness to stay at that capital was also discerned. Taking all this into consideration therefore, an edict was issued, directing His Royal Highness to deliver up Balkh and Badakhshan to Nazar Muhammad Khan, provided the latter would come and have an interview with him, and then set out with all the victorious forces for Hindustan, the type of Paradise.

Cession of Balkh and Badakhshan to Nazar Muhammad Khan, and Retreat of Aurangzeb

. . . . On the 4th of the month of Ramazan, early in the morning, which was the time selected for Nazar Muhammad Khan's interview, news came in that he had sent his grandson Muhammad Kasim, son of Khusru Sultan, in company with Kafsh Kalmak and several chiefs, and that they had all advanced two *kos* beyond the bridge of Khatab. The Prince, appreciating the gradations of rank, deputed his son, Mohammad Sultan, along with Bahadur Khan and some other nobles, to go and meet him; and that early fruit of the orchard of royalty having dutifully obeyed the command, brought the individual in question into his noble father's presence. The Prince, well versed in etiquette, then folded Muhammad Kasim in a fond embrace, and placed him in an adjoining seat; after which Kafsh Kalmak delivered the Khan's letter, full of apologies for not having come in consequence of an attack of indisposition, and represented that the Khan, being obliged to forego the pleasure of an interview, had sent Muhammad Kasim as his representative, with a view to remove all suspicion of his having wilfully broken his promise.

After dismissing Muhammad Kasim, the Prince addressed the commanders of the army in that country, *viz*. . . . . saying, his instructions were, to deliver over Balkh and Badakhshan to Nazar Muhammad Khan, after the interview; but now that the latter had only sent his grandson, excusing himself on the pretended plea of sickness, he could not carry out this measure without a distinct order. He told them to take into consideration, however, that the country was desolated, winter close at hand, grain scarce, and time short; so that there would be great difficulty in making arrangements for the winter, and remaining in the kingdom during that inclement season, and asked them what was their opinion on the subject. The principal chiefs replied, that the passes of the Hindu Koh were just about to be covered by snow, when the road would be blocked up; so that, if he reported the matter, and waited the arrival of instructions, the opportunity would slip through his hands. They therefore came to the unanimous conclusion, that His Royal Highness should recall all the governors of forts and persons in charge of places around Balkh.

As a vast number of mercenary soldiers, consisting of Uzbeks and Almans, had crossed the river Jihun, and spread themselves over those regions, and wherever they saw a concourse of people, took the first opportunity of assailing them, Raja Jai Singh was despatched to Turmuz to fetch Sa'adat Khan. The Prince was also on the point of starting off Bahadur Khan to bring back Rustam Khan from Andkhod, and Shad Khan from Maimanah, so that they might rejoin the army in safety. In the interim, however, a letter arrived from Rustam Khan, saying, that as he had ascertained that the country was to be delivered up to Nazar Muhammad Khan, he had set out from Andkhod to Maimanah, with the intention of taking Shad Khan from thence in company with him, and proceeding towards Kabul by way of Sancharik. The Prince then marched with all the royal forces from the neighbourhood of Faizabad, and encamped at Chalkai, which lies contiguous to the city of Balkh; where, having ceded the country to Nazar Muhammad Khan, he delivered up the town and citadel of Balkh to Muhammad Kasim and Kafsh Kalmak. He presented the former of these, on bidding him farewell, with a jewelled dagger, a horse caparisoned with golden trappings, and 50,000 rupees out of the royal treasury. He also committed to his charge, among the stores contained in the fort and city, 50,000 *mans* of grain belonging to His Majesty, which, estimated by the rate ruling at that time, was worth five *lacs* of rupees; and besides this, all the granaries of the other forts. At this stage, Mirza Raja Jai Singh returned from Turmuz, accompanied by Sa'adat Khan, and joined the army. From the beginning of the invasion of Balkh and Badakhshan till the end, when those conquered territories were ceded to Nazar Muhammad Khan, there was expended out of the State exchequer, in the progress of this undertaking, the sum of two *krors* of rupees, which is equivalent to seven *lacs* of the *tumans* current in Irak.

To be brief, on the 14th of the aforesaid month of Ramazan, the Prince started from Chalkai with all the royal forces for Kabul. He appointed Amiru-l Umara with a party to form the left wing; Mirza Raja Jai Singh with his, the right; and Bahadur Khan the rear-guard; whilst he sent on Mu'tamad Khan, the *Mir-i atish*, with the whole of the royal artillerymen, and Pirthi Raj Rathor, as a vanguard; so that the bands of Uzbeks, ever watching for an opportunity of attack, might not be able to harass and cut off the stragglers in the rear of the army, whilst winding through the narrow defiles and passes. As it was an arduous task for the whole army to cross the pass of 'Arbang in one day, the victorious Prince himself having marched through it safely, waited on the further side with Amiru-l Umara, till the entire army was over; and by His Royal Highness's order, Bahadur Khan halted at the mouth of the above pass, for the sake of helping the camp and baggage through. He was also in the habit of sending some of the troops every day to protect the party who went out to fetch grass and firewood. One day, when the turn for this duty came to Shamsher Khan, Khushhal Beg Kashghari, and others of his countrymen, the Uzbeks, imagining the party to be a small one, advanced, to the number of about 5,000 horsemen, and one moiety of them having encompassed Shamsher Khan and his comrades in the midst, the other took up a position on the summit of some eminences. Bahadur Khan, having received intimation of this, went to his support, and having made several of those marauders a prey to the sword of vengeance, put the remainder to flight; whilst out of the royal troops some few were wounded. On the third day of the halt, whilst the rest of the army were crossing the pass of 'Arbang, a body of Almans made their appearance; whereupon Nazar Bahadur Khan, Kheshji Ratan son of Muhesh Das, and some others, charged them on one side, and on the other Mu'tamad Khan with the artillerymen, and a number of the Prince's retainers. The enemy, unable to withstand the shock, turned and fled, closely pursued by the royalists, who killed and wounded a few of them.

SHAH JAHAN-NAMA

The day they had to march from Ghori by way of Khwaja Zaid, as the road to the next stage, which had been selected on the banks of the Surkhab, was extremely difficult, and there was a great likelihood of an attack from the Uzbeks and Hazaras, the Prince left Amiru-l Umara at the top of the aforesaid pass, to protect the men who used to follow in rear of the army. As there was an interval of two *kos* between Amiru-l Umara, Bahadur Khan, and the left wing of the army, a portion of the baggage, whlist treading the road, was plundered by the Hazaras. A vast body of them also fell upon the treasure; but Zu-l Kadar Khan, and the rest who were with it, firmly held their ground, and the battle was warmly contested till some part of the night was spent. Amiru-l Umara, having been informed of the circumstance, sent a detachment of his own men to their assistance; whereupon the enemy retreated in confusion. After the camp had advanced beyond Shaburghan, during the march to Nek Bihar and to Char-chashma, some injury accrued to the troops, in consequence of the narrowness and steepness of the road, and the rolling over of several laden beasts of burden, which were accidentally led along the top of the hill off the path by by some of the people who had lost their way. When they started from *Char-chashma* for the foot of the Hindu Koh range, it was resolved, for the greater convenience of the troops, that the Prince should first cross the pass, and at the expiration of a day Amiru-l Umara should follow; that after him should come the royal treasure, *kar-khana* (wardrobe) and artillery, with all His Royal Highness s establishment; and in this way, a party having gradually crossed every day, Bahadur Khan, who occupied the rear of the victorious army, should follow last of all. The illustrious Prince, having reached the foot of the pass that day, passed over the Hindu Koh on the next, and though the weather was not intensely cold, yet as snow had fallen previously, and there was a hard frost, the men got over with considerable difficulty.

On the morrow, the Prince reached Ghorband, whence he marched during the night into Kabul. When Amiru-l Umara, who followed one days' march in rear, was encamped at the foot of the pass, at midnight it began to snow, and continued doing without intermission till morning; after which the weather became fair, and the Amir having got through the pass with his force, entered Kabul two days after His Royal Highness. As for Raja Jai Singh, who, the day the camp marched from Surkhab, had stayed behind by the Prince's orders at the place, on account of the narrowness of the road, and the difficulty of the defiles that occurred further on, as soon as he passed Char-chashma, the snow commenced falling, and never once ceased all that day and the next, during which he halted on the road. After arriving at the pass of the Hindu Koh, till crossing over it, the snow kept falling for three more days and nights; and Zu-l Kadar Khan, whose duty it was to guard the treasure. seeing, when four *kos* distant from the Hindu Koh, that a snow-storm was coming on, started at once in the hope of getting the treasure through the pass, before it could have time to stop up the road. It chanced, however, that the snow gradually accumulated to such a depth, that most of the camels tumbled down, and nearly half of them were rendered quite unserviceable, so that the Khan in question, despite his utmost exertions, was unable to cross that day. In consequence of the intense cold, his comrades, both horse and foot, got dispersed, and saving a few servants of the crown, no one remained with him; nevertheless he stayed on the summit of the ridge, to guard the treasure, nothwithstanding the snow-storm. In the morning, having laden a portion of it on such of the camels as were capable of travelling, he started it off in advance to Ghorband, escorted by some of the horsemen; whilst he himself with a few others occupied themselves in guarding the remainder, and spent sveen days and nights on the top of the Hindu

Koh in the midst of snow and intense cold, and with but a scanty supply of provisions, waiting for Bahadur Khan's arrival, who was behind. The fortunes of the latter were as follows. As soon as he reached the pass of Nek Bihar, which is two marches from the Hindu Koh, and has a very precipitous descent, the snow began to fall, and continued coming down all night till twelve o'clock next day. Owing to the difficulties of the pass, which were greatly enhanced by the heavy fall of snow, he only got the rest of the camp and army through with immense labour. At this juncture, the malicious Hazaras, in their eager desire for plunder, assaulted the camp followers more desperately than every but Bahadur Khan each time inflicted summary chastisement on the free-booters, and drove them off. After reaching the foot of the Hindu Koh pass, and halting there for a day, he sent on all those who had lagged in the rear, and as soon as they were across, set out himself. As most of the people spent the night on the summit of the pass, on account of the difficult roads, and the intense coldness of a mountain climate, heightened by the deep snow and chilling blasts, some of the men and cattle that were worn out and infirm perished. Accordingly, from the first commencement of the army's crossing to the end, about 5,000 men, and a similar number of animals, such as horses, elephants, camels, oxen, etc., were destroyed, and a vast deal of property remained buried in the snow. When Bahadur Khan came to the top of the pass, and Zu-l Kadar Khan explained the state of affairs to him, he halted there, and in company with Ikhlas Khan, and some other nobles and *mansabdars* who still stood by him, spent the night on the spot. In the morning, having thrown the baggage off all such of his own camels as he could find, he loaded them with the treasure, and distributed the rest among the horses and camels belonging to the troops. Just as he was on the point of starting, a body of Hazaras came up in the rear, and seeing the paucity of his detachment, resolved upon makin an assault, for the sake of carrying off the treasure. Bahadur Khan, however, faced about, and made some of the doomed wretches a prey to (the crocodile of) his bloodthirsty sword, and routed the remainder. He then set out with the treasure, and reached Balkh along with his comrades, after an interval of fourteen days from the time of the Prince's arrival there.

Despatch of a Candlestick to the Glorious City.

Among the events of this year was the despatch of a candlestick studded with gems to the revered tomb of the Prophet (on whom be the greatest favours, and blessings!) an account of which is here given. Some time previous to this it was represented that a wonderfully large diamond from a mine in the territory of Golkonda had fallen into the hands of Kutbu-l Mulk; whereupon an order was issued, directing him to forward the same to Court; when its estimated value would be taken into account, as part of the two *lacs* of *huns* (pagodas), which was the stipulated amount of his annual tribute. He accordingly sent the diamond in question, which weighed in its rough state 180 *ratis,* to Court; and after His Majesty's own lapidaries had cut away as much of the outer surface as was requisite to disclose all its beauties, there remained a rare gem of 100 *ratis* weight, valued by the jewellers at one *lac* and 50,000 rupees. As such a valuable diamond as this had never been brought to the threshold, resembling the Elysian abode, since his accession to the throne, the pious monarch, the bulwark of religion, with the best intention, and the utmost sincerity of purpose, made a vow to send it to the pure sepulchre of the last of the Prophets (*on whom be peace*!). Having therefore selected out of the amber candlesticks that he had amongst his private property the largest of them all, which weighed 700 *tolas,* and was worth 10,000 rupees, he commanded that it should be covered with a network of gold, ornamented on all sides with flowers, and studded with gums, among which that valuable diamond should also be included.

In short, that incomparable candlestick cost two *lacs* and 50,000 rupees, of which one *lac* and 50,000 was the price of the diam ıd, and the remaining *lac* the worth of all the gems and gold, together with the original candlestick. Mir Saiyid Ahamad Sa'id Bahari, who had once before conveyed charitable presents tɔ the two sacred cities, was then deputed to take charge of this precious offering; and an edict was promulgated to the effect, that the revenue collectors of the province of Gujarat should purchase a *lac* and 60,000 rupees worth of goods for the sacred fane, and deliver it over to him, so that he might take it along with him from thence. Out of this, he was directed to present 50,000 rupees worth to the Sharif of Mecca; to sell 60,000 rupees worth, and distribute the proceeds, together with any profit that might accrue, amongst the indigent of that sacred city; and the remaining 50,000, in like manner, amongst those of the glorious Medina. The above-named Saiyid, who was only in receipt of a daily stipend, was promoted to a suitable *mansab,* and having been munificently presented with a dress of onour and a donation of 12,000 rupees, received his ismissal.

ACCOUNT OF THE FOUNDING OF THE FORT AT THE METROPOLIS OF SHAH-JAHANABAD

The following is an exact account of the founding of the splendid fort in the above-named metropolis, with its edifices resembling Paradise, which was constructed in the environs of the city of Dehli, on the banks of the river Jumna. It first occurred to the omniscient mind that he should select on the banks of the aforesaid river some pleasant site, distinguished by its genial climate, where he might found a splendid fort and delightful edifices, agreeably to the promptings of his generous heart, through which streams of water should be made to flow, and the terraces of which should overlook the river. When, after a long search, a piece of ground outside of the city of Dehli, lying between the most distant suburbs and Nurgarh, commonly called Salimgarh, was fixed upon for this purpose, by the royal command, on the night of Friday, the 25th of Zi-l hijja, in the twelfth year of his auspicious reign, corresponding to 1048 A.H., being the time appointed by the astrologers, the foundations were marked out with the usual ceremonies, according to the plan devised, in the august presence. Active labourers were then employed in digging the foundations, and on the night of Friday, the 9th of Muharram, of the year coinciding with 1049 A.H. (1639 A.D.), the foundation-stone of that noble structure was laid. Throughout the Imperial dominions, wherever artificers could be found, whether plain stone-cutters, ornamental sculptors, masons, or carpenters, by the mandate worthy of implicit obedience, they were all collected together, and multitudes of common labourers were employed in the work. It was ultimately completed on the 24th of Rabi'u-l awwal, in the twenty-first year of his reign, corresponding to 1058 A.H., at an outlay of 60 *lacs* of rupees, after taking nine years three months and some days in building.

FIROZ SHAH'S CANAL

The canal that Sultan Firoz Shah Khilji, during the time he reigned at Dehli, had made to branch off from the river Jumna, in the vicinity of *pargana* Khizrabad, whence he brought it in a channel 30 Imperial *kos* long to the confines of *pargana* Safidun, which was his hunting-seat, and had only a scanty supply of water, had, after the Sultan's death, become in the course of time ruinous. Whilst Shahabu-d din Ahmad Khan held the government of Dehli, during the reign of the Emperor Akbar, he put it in repair and set it flowing again, with a view to fertilize the places in his *jagir*, and hence it was called Nahr-i Shahab; but for want of repairs, however, it again stopped flowing. At the time when the sublime attention was turned to the building of this fort and palace, it was commanded that the aforesaid canal from Khizrabad to Safidun should be repaired, and a new channel excavated from the latter spot to the regal residence, which also is a distance of 30 Imperial *kos*. After it was thus prolonged, it was designated the Nahr-i Bihisht.

TWENTY-SECOND YEAR OF THE REIGN, 1058 A.H. (1648 A.D.)

Advance of the Persians against Kandahar—Despatch of an army thither

On the 22nd of the month of Ramazan, when the standards of prosperity, after their return from Safidun, were planted at His Majesty's private hunging-seat, it reached the ear of royalty, through the representations of Daulat Khan, ruler of Kandahar, and Purdil Khan, governor of fort Bust, that Shah 'Abbas the Second, having come to the sacred city of Tus (*Mashhad-i Mukaddas*), with intent to rescue the kingdom of Kandahar, had proceeded towards the confines of Khurasan, with all his matchlockmen[3] and pioneers. It was, besides, reported that he had despatched men to Farah, Sistan, and other places; to collect supplies of grain, and having sent on a party in advance to Hirat, was doing his utmost to block up the road on this side; being well aware that, during the winter, owing to the quantity of snow on the ground, the arrival of reinforcements from Hindustan by way of Kabul and Multan was impracticable, he proposed advancing in this direction during that inclement season, and had despatched Shah Kuli Beg, son of Maksud Beg, his *wazir*, as expeditiously as possible, with a letter to Court, and further that the

[3] *The word which Major Fuller translates is "tufangchi."*

individual in question had reached Kandahar, and without halting more than three days, had resumed his journey to the august presence.

His Majesty, after hearing this intelligence, having summoned 'Allami Sa'du-lla Khan from the metropolis, commanded him to write *farmans* to all the nobles and *mansabdars* who were at their respective estates, *jagirs*, and homes, directing them to set out with all speed for Court. It was likewise ordered that the astrologers should determine the proper moment for the departure of the world-traversing camp from the metropolis to the capitals Lahore and Kabul.

APPOINTMENT OF PRINCE MUHAMMAD AURANGZEB BAHADUR, 'ALLAMI SA'DU-LLA KHAN, ETC., TO LEAD THE ARMY AGAINST KANDAHAR

As soon as it reached the royal ear, through Daulat Khan's representations, that on the 10th of Ẕi-l hijja, the Shah had arrived outside the fortress of Kandahar, and besieged it, the ever-successful Prince Muhammad Aurangzeb Bahadur was appointed to proceed thither with 'Allami Sa'du-lla Khan, and some of the chief officers of State, such as Bahadur Khan, Mirza Raja Jai Singh, Rustam Khan, Raja Bithaldas, and Kalich Khan. Besides these, there were upwards of fiifty individuals from amongst the nobles, and a vast number of *mansabdars, ahadi* archers, and matchlockmen—the whole number of whom, under the regulation requiring them to bring one-fifth of their respective tallies of fighting men into the field, would amount to 50,000 horsemen, and according to the rule enforcing a fourth, to 60,000—as well as 10,000 infantry, matchlock and rocket men, etc. It was ordered that subsidiary grants of money out of the State exchequer should be made to the nobles and *mansabdars* holding *jagirs*, who were appointed to serve in this expedition, at the rate of 100 rupees for every individual horseman, which would be a *lac* for every hundred; that to those who drew pecuniary stipends in place of holding *jagirs*, three month's pay in advance should be disbursed; and in like manner also to the *ahadis* and matchlockmen, who numbered 5,000 horse, should a similar advance be made; so that they might not suffer any privations during the campaign from want of funds to meet their current expenses.

On the 18th of the month of Muharram, it being a fortunate moment, 'Allami was dismissed alongwith the nobles who were present in His Majesty's fortunate train, and *farmans* were issued to those who were staying in the province of Kabul and other places, to join the royal forces at once. Various marks of favour and regard were manifested towards 'Allami and his associates, on their taking leave, by the bestowal of *khil'ats*, jewelled daggers, and swords, horses, and elephants on them, according to their different grades of rank. He also forwarded by the hands of 'Allami for the gallant Prince—to whom an order had been issued previous to this, directing him to start instantly from Multan and overtake the royal forces at Bhimbhar—a handsome *khil'at*. . . . It was further commanded that the ever-victorious army should hasten to Kabul *via* Bangash-i bala and Bangash-i payin, as they were the shortest routes, and thence proceed by way of Ghazni towards Kandahar.

LOSS OF KANDAHAR

On the 8th of Rabi'u-l awwal, when the victorious camp started from Jahangirabad, intelligence reached the Court that the servants of the crown had lost possession of the fortresses of Kandahar and Bust, and all the rest in that country; a detailed account of which events is here given. When Shah 'Abbas came from Tus to Hirat, he proceeded from thence to Farah; where, having halted some days, he marched upon Kandahar, having, however, first despatched Mihrab Khan with some of his nobles, and an additional number of matchlockmen, etc.,

'INAYAT KHAN

amounting altogether to about 8,000 horsemen, to besiege the fortress of Bust, and Saz Khan Baligh with five or six thousand composed of Kazalbashis and the troops of Karki and Naksari,[1] to subdue Zamindawar. On reaching that place, he fixed his head-quarters in the garden of Ganj Kuli Khan, whilst Kaulat Khan, who had shut himself up in the fortress, having committed the interior of the stronghold to the charge of trusty persons, appointed a party of the royal matchlockmen and a portion of his own men to occupy the summit of Kambul Hill. The defence of the towers he left to the care of Kakar Khan, to whom he also sent some of the matchlockmen; and the protection of the intrenchments below the Bashuri and Khwaja Khizr gates he entrusted to Nur-l Hasan, *bakhshi* of *ahadis*, with a body of the latter who were serving under him. He also appointed some of the household troops, and a number of matchlockmen belonging to the Kandahar levies, to garrison the fortifications of Daulatabad and Mandavi, and having consigned the superintendence of them to Mirak Husain, *bakhshi* of Kandahar, came himself from the citadel to the former of these two forts, for the purpose of looking after the intrenchments. With a wanton disregard to the dictates of prudence, however, he did not attend to the defence of the towers, that Kalich Khan, in the days of his administration, had constructed expressly for such an occasion, on the top of the hill of Chihal-Zinah (forty steps), whence guns and matchlocks could be fired with effect into the forts of Daulatabad and Mandavi. The Kazalbashis, therefore, seeing those towers devoid of protection, despatched a number of matchlockmen to take post in them, and open a destructive fire. They also laid out intrenchments in different quarters. . . .

At length a number of the garrison, from want of

[1] *Variously written and doubtful.*

spirit, lost the little courage they possessed, and Shadi Uzbek having entered into a conspiracy with the Kazalbashis, seduced Kipchak Khan from his duty. Though the latter was not naturally inclined at heart to this course of behaviour, yet as his companions had their families with them, through dread of losing their wealth, their lives, and their good repute, they would not let him follow the bent of his own disposition, so he was necessarily compelled to ally himself with those unfortunates. Some of the Mughal *mansabdars, ahadis,* and matchlockmen too, having sprinkled the dust of treason on the heads of loyalty, entered into a league with them, and having come in front of the fort, declared that, in consequence of all the roads being closed, from the vast quantity of snow on the ground, there was no hope of the early arrival of succour, and that it was evident from the untiring efforts of the Kazalbashis, that they would very shortly capture the fort, and after its reduction by force and violence, neither would there be any chance of their own lives being spared, nor of their offspring being saved from captivity. The wretched Daulat Khan, who ought instantly to have extinguished the flames of this sedition with the water of the sword, showed an utter want of spirit, by contenting himself with offering advice in reply. This, however, made no impression on the individuals in question, who got up, and departed to their respective homes, so that nought but a scanty force being left in the intrenchments, the Kazalbashis entered the Sher-Haji in several places. As for the party that forced an entrance on the side of the Babawali gate, some of the household troops and Daulat Khan's followers, who occupied that quarter, rushed upon them, whereupon several were killed on both sides.

Meanwhile, the traitor Shadi sent a message to the governor of the fort, who was stationed at the above gate, to say that Muhammad Beg Baki had come, bearing a letter and message from the Shah, and accompanied by Sharafu-d din Husain, a *mansabdar* who was *darogha* of the buildings and magazines in the fort of Bust. Daulat Khan, on this, despatched Mirak Husain Bakhshi, for the purpose of sending away Muhammad Beg from the gate; but as soon as the *bakhshi* reached the gate of Veskaran, he noticed Kipchak Khan, Shadi, and a number of the Mughal *mansabdars,* sitting in the gateway, and perceived that they had brought Muhammad Beg inside, and seated him in front of them, and that he had brought four letters, one addressed to Daulat Khan, and the other three to Shadi, Nuru-l Hasan and Mirak Husain, and was saying that he had besides some verbal messages to deliver. Mirak Husain therefore turned back, and related the circumstances to Daulat Khan; whereupon that worthless wretch deputed his *Lashkar-navis* (paymaster of the forces) to detain Muhammad Beg there, and send Kipchak Khan, and Shadi to him. As soon as these ungrateful wretches came, acting in confomity with their advice, he adopted the contemptible resolution of proceeding to an interview with Muhammad Beg, and receiving and keeping the letters he brought. The Shah also sent a message to the effect, that he should take warning from what had already befallen Purdil Khan, the governor of the fort of Bust, and his comrades; and neither prolong hostilities any further, nor strive to shed the blood and sully the fair fame of himself and his comrades; and with a view to acquaint the inmates of the fort with the condition of the garrison of Bust, he despatched along with Muhammad Beg the aforesaid Sharafu-d din Husain, whom Mihrab Khan had started off loaded with chains in advance of himself. To this Daulat Khan replied, that he would return an answer five days hence; and it having been stipulated that during this interval hostilities should not be engaged in on either side, Muhammad Beg received his dismissal, and returned to his own camp.

On the 5th day 'Ali Kuli Khan, brother of Rustam Khan, the former commander-in-chief, having come to

Shadi's intrechment, and delivered a message, saying that the Shah had commissioned him to ascertain their final decision, the pusillanimous Daulat Khan, with most of the servants of the crown, went to the gate, and invited him in. The latter, after being introduced, stated, that as they had already offered as gallant and stubborn a resistance as it was possible to make, it was now proper that they should refrain from fighting, and, applying themselves to the preservation of their lives and property, should send an individual along with him to deliver their reply. The worthless Daulat Khan accordingly despatched 'Abdu-l Latif, *diwan* of Kandahar, for the purpose of procuring a safe conduct, in company with the above individual, and on the following day he returned with the written agreement.

The villain Shadi, however, without waiting for the governor's evacuating the fort, surrendered the Veskaran gate, which was in his charge, during the night to the Kazalbashis, and hastened along with Kipchak Khan to the Shah's camp. However much the miserable Daulat Khan exhorted his men to repair to the fort on the top of the hill, it was of no avail; though had he but taken shelter there with a detachment, he could have held out till the arrival of succour without suffering any harm. On the morrow, when the *mansabdars, ahadis,* and matchlockmen, who were engaged in the defence of the gates of the new and old forts, marched out, after obtaining a safe conduct, with the exception of the citadel where the helpless Daulat Khan was left with Kakar Khan, the base Raja Amar Singh, and some other *mansabdars,* as well as a party of his own adherents, every spot was in the possession of the Kazalbashis.

On the 9th of Safar, this year, 'Ali Kuli Khan came and said that any longer delay could not be permitted; whereupon the disloyal Daulat Khan delivered up a place of refuge of that description, and having marched out with his goods and comrades, encamped at a distance of a *kos*. During the period of the siege, which extended over two months, nearly 2,000 of the Kazalbash army and 400 of the garrison were slain.

Summarily, on the third day after Daulat Khan's dastardly evacuation of the fort, 'Ali Kuli Khan, Isa Khan, and his brother Jamshid Khan, came to him, and intimated that the Shah had sent for him, as well as for some of his chief officers and associates. The latter replied that it would be better for them to excuse him from this trouble, or, if they were resolved upon taking him there, to manage so that there should be no delay in his getting his dismissal, and to give him a dress of honour, both of which requests were guaranteed by 'Ali Kuli Khan. The ill-fated Daulat Khan accordingly proceeded with Kakar Khan and Nuru-l Hasan, in company with the above-named nobles, to wait upon the Shah, and having received his dismissal after a few moments, returned to his own camp, and on the 18th of the month of Safar set out with a world of shame and ignominy for Hindustan.

The Shah, in consequence of the horses with his army having mostly perished for want of forage, in addition to which a scarcity of grain was experienced, appointed Mihrab Khan, with about 10,000 Kazalbashis and slaves, armed with matchlocks, to garrison Kandahar; and Dost 'Ali Uzbek with a detachment to guard the fortress of Bust, and returned himself to Khurasan on the 24th of this month. The account of the fortress of Bust is as follows. . .

SURRENDER OF BUST

From the beginning of the siege, the flames of war and strife raged furiously for 54 days, and many were killed and wounded on both sides; insomuch that during this period close upon 600 of the Kazalbashis, and nearly half that number of Purdil Khan's followers, met their death. On the 14th Muharram, this year, the governor having begged for quarter, after entering into a strict agreement, had an interview with Mihrab Khan. The latter, having broken his engagement, put to death out of the 600 men, who had stood by the governor to the last, several persons, who being averse to the surrender, had protracted the struggle; and having made that individual himself a prisoner, together with the rest of his adherents, and his family and children, brought them all to the Shah at Kandahar.

In Zamindawar the war was carried on as follows. As soon as Saz Khan Baligh besieged the fort, Saiyid Asadu-lla, and Saiyid Bakar, sons of Saiyid Bayazid Bukhari, who were engaged in its defence, sent him a message, saying that the fort was a dependency of Kandahar, and without reducing the latter, its capture would be of no use; and it would therefore be better to suspend hostilities until the fate of Kandahar was ascertained, so that blood might not be shed fruitlessly. Saz Khan, concurring in the reasonableness of this proposition, refrained from prosecuting siege operations, and having written to inform the Shah of the fact, sat down to await intelligence. A messenger from the Shah at length brought to the Saiyids a letter, detailing the capture of the fortresses of Bust and Kandahar; whereupon they surrendered the fort.

ADVANCE OF THE IMPERIAL ARMY TO KANDAHAR

The exploits of the royal army were as follows. The day that 'Allami Sa'du-lla Khan crossed the Nilab with the royal forces, Prince Muhammad Aurangzeb Bahadur having arrived from Multan, also effected his passage over the river; and the whole of the forces set out at once in His Royal Highness's train for Kohat. On reaching that place, he halted to await the receipt of intelligence regarding the snow; and presently a letter arrived from Khalil Beg, who had been sent on in advance to level the road and construct bridges, to the effect that on the road through the hill-country along the Kohistan route the snow was lying so deep that even if no more fell, the road would not probably be passable for at least a month. The ever-victorious Prince consequently relinquished his design of proceeding by that route, but started in the direction of Peshawar, by way of the pass of Sendh-Basta, which is an extremely rugged and difficult road, and without entering that city, pursued his journey by the regular stages to Kabul. . . .

Sa'du-lla Khan having set out with his comrades at full speed, came and pitched camp during the night in the suburbs of Shahr Safa. Having left Mubarak Khan Niazi to guard that city, he marched thence, and in three days reached the neighbourhood of Kandahar, on the 12th of Jumada-l awwal of this year; whence Kasadah Khwaja, which is half a *kos* from the fortress, became the site of his camp. As the 14th of the above-named month was the time fixed upon for commencing the siege, he halted next day to await the arrival of the victorious Prince, and the advent of the appointed time for the siege, but rode out in company with the commanders of the royal forces, and made a reconnoitring tour round the fortifications. On the 14th the Prince came up from the rear, and having joined the army, fixed his headquarters half a *kos* from the fortress. . . .

TWENTY-THIRD YEAR OF THE REIGN, 1059 A.H. (1649 A.D.)

As it was represented that during the progress of the victorious forces towards Kandahar a great deal of the cultivation of Ghazni and its dependencies had been trodden under foot by the army, the merciful monarch, the cherisher of his people, despatched the sum of 2000 gold *mohurs*, in charge of a trusty individual, with directions to inquire into the loss sustained by the argiculturists, and distribute it amongst them accordingly.

After the fortress of Kandahar had been besieged for three months and a half, so that grain and fodder were beginning to get scarce, notwithstanding the praiseworthy exertions of the faithful servants of the crown, owing to their having with them neither a siege train of battering guns, nor skilful artillerymen, the capture of the fortress seemed as distant as ever. For these reasons, and as the winter also was close at hand, a *farman* was issued to the illustrious Prince, to the effect that, as the reduction of the fortress without the aid of heavy guns was impracticable, and there was not now sufficient time remaining for them to arrive in, he should defer its capture till a more convenient opportunity, and start for Hindustan with the victorious troops. The Prince Buland Ikbal Dara Shukoh was also ordered to tarry some time at Kabul, and rirectly he heard the news of the Kandahar army's arrival at Ghazni, to set out for the presence. . .

As the winter was now close at hand, and forage had become unattainable, notwithstanding hearing of the death of Mihrab Khan, the *kiladar,* from a number of persons, who came out of the fortress, the Prince did not deem it expedient to delay any longer, but, in obedience to the mandate worthy of all attention, set out with the victorious forces from Kandahar on the 8th of the month of Ramazan this year for Hindustan. . .

TWENTY-FOURTH OF THE REIGN, 1060 A.H. (1650 A.D.)

The Emperor Excused The Fast

As his most gracious Majesty had this year advanced in joy and prosperity beyond the age of sixty, and the divine precepts sanctioning the non-observance of the fast came into force, the learned doctors and *muftis,* according to the glorious ordinances of the Kuran, by way of fulfilling the commandments of the law, decreed that it would be lawful for His Majesty, whose blessed person is the source of the administration of the world, to expend funds in charity in lieu of observing the fast. The monarch, the lover of religion, and worshipper of the divine law, therefore, lavished 60,000 rupees on the deserving poor; and at his command, every night during the sacred month divers viands and all sorts of sweet-meats were laid out in the Chihalsitun in front of the balcony of public audience, with which famishing and destitute people appeased their hunger. It was further resolved that henceforward a similar plan should be pursued during every month of Ramazan.

TWENTY-FIFTH YEAR OF THE REIGN, 1061 A.H. (1650-1 A.D.)

Subjugation of Tibet

On the 23rd Jumada-s sani, which was the time fixed for entering Kashmir, the Emperor alighted in safety at the royal apartments of the fort.

On the 4th of Rajab His Majesty paid a visit to the Mosque, which had been erected in the most exquisite style of art, for the asylum of learning, Mulla Shah Badakhshani, at a cost of 40,000 rupees, the requisite funds having been provided by Nawab 'Aliya, and was surrounded by buildings to serve as habitations for the poor, which were constructed at a further outlay of 20,000 rupees.

On the 12th of this month, Adam Khan's *munshi* and his nephew Muhammad Murad, as well as the sons of Salim Beg Kashghari, who ranked amongst the auxiliaries serving in the province of Kashmir, and had stood security for the two former individuals, were appointed to proceed to Tibet, with a number of *zamindars,* to exterminate a rebel named Mirza Jan, and subdue the fort of Shkardu, together with the territory of Tibet, which had escaped out of the possession of the servants of the crown.

On the 27th of Sha'ban it reached the ear replete with all good, through Adam Khan's representations, that the rebel Mirza Jan had no sooner heard of the arrival of the royaltists, then he evacuated the fort of Shkardu, and became a wanderer in the desert of adversity; whereupon the fort in question, together with the territory of Tibet, came anew into the possession of the servants of the crown. The gracious monarch rewarded the aforesaid Khan with an addition to his *mansab*, and conferred the country of Tibet in *jagir* on the above-named Muhammad Murad, as his fixed abode.

Towards the close of the spring, on account of the heavy rain and tremendous floods, all the verdant islands in the middle of the Dal, as well as the gardens along its borders, and those in the suburbs of the city, were shorn of their grace and loveliness. The waters of the Dal rose to such a height, that they even poured into the garden below the balcony of public audience, which became one sheet of water from the rush of the foaming tide, and most of its trees were swamped. Just about this time, too, a violent hurricane of wind arose, which tore up many trees, principally poplars and planes, by the roots, in all the gardens, and hurled down from on high all the blooming foliage of Kashmir. A longer sojourn in that region was consequently distasteful to the gracious mind; so, notwithstanding that the sky was lowering, he quitted Kashmir on the 1st of Ramazan, and set out for the capital by way of Shahabad.

PROGRESS TO KABUL, AND DESPATCH OF 'ALLAMI SA'DU-LLA KHAN WITH AN IMMENSE ARMY FOR THE SUBJUGATION OF KANDAHAR

On the night of Monday, the 18th of Rabi'u-l awwal, being the moment that had been fixed for the auspicious departure to Kabul, the royal train moved from the capital of Lahore in that direction. At the same chosen period, too, His Majesty despatched 'Allami with the multitudinous forces (resembling the waves of the sea), amounting together with the army serving in Kabul to 50,000 cavalry and 10,000 infantry, including musketeers, gunners, bombardiers, and rocketmen, for the purpose of conquering the country and fortress of Kandahar, Bust and Zamindawar. He was further accompanied by ten large and ferocious war-elephants, eight heavy and twenty light guns; the latter of which carried two and two and a half *sir* (four and five lbs.) shot, and during an engagement used to be advanced in front of the army; twenty elephants carrying *hathnals,* and 100 camels with *shuturnals,* besides a well-replenished treasury, and other suitable equipments. He was instructed to repair by way of Kabul and Ghazni to Kandahar, and about 3,000 camels were employed in the transport of artillery stores. such as lead, powder and iron shot. . .

TWENTY-SIXTH YEAR OF THE REIGN. 1062 A.H. (1651-2 A.D.)

Arrival of Prince Muhammad Aurangzeb Bahadur and Jamdatu-l Mulk Sa'Du-lla Khan at Kandahar, and siege of the fortress

On the 3rd of Jumada-s sani, the first month this year, the victorious Prince Muhammad Aurangzeb Bahadur, who had set out from Multan for Kandahar, reached his destination. 'Allami. who had hastened thither by way of Kabul, having joined His Royal Highness on the above date, delivered the kind and indulgent *farman*. As it had been determined that the siege of the fortress should be commenced simultaneously with the arrival at Kandahar, the fortunate Prince, having finished marking out the positions that the royal forces were to occupy. invested the stronghold that very day. . . .

In short, for two months and eight days the flames of war burned fiercely. and on both sides numerous casualties occurred. On one occasion, when Muhammad Beg *Topchi-bashi* (Commandant of the Artillery), and five or six others of the garrison, had been destroyed by a shot from the gun named Fath Lashkar, the Kazalbashis sallied out of the fort and poured down upon the trenches; whereupon a desperate struggle ensued between the adverse hosts. Another time they fell on 'Allami's trenches: but a party of his retainers firmly held their ground, and after putting a few of their antagonists to the sword, and wounding some others, manfully laid down their lives; and on the arrival of succour, the enemy retired precipitately within the fortifications.

To be brief, the royalists used the most strenuous exertions, and laboured with unremitting zeal and assiduity in carrying forward the parallels and zigags of attack, and demolishing the crest of the parapet and the bastions. Nevertheless, as the fortress possessed immense strength, and was filled with all the military weapons and stores required for an effective defence, their utmost efforts produced no impression, and, owing to the storm of shot and shell that poured on them like a shower of rain from the fort, they were unable to advance their trenches beyond the spot they had already brought them to. In the interim, out of the seven guns which had accompanied the royal army, and were the most effectual implements of attack, two that were mounted in the Prince's trenches had cracked from constant firing, and had become quite unserviceable. As for the other five, which were in the trenches conducted by 'Allami and Kasim Khan *Mir-i atish,* although they continued to be discharged, yet as they were not served by scientific artillerymen, their fire was not so effective as could be wished.

As soon as these particulars became known to His Majesty's world-adorning understanding, and he was informed that the capture of the fortress was at that period impracticable; and it also reached the royal ear that the Uzbeks and Almans had come into the neighbourhood of Ghazni, and excited tumults, as already described, a *arman* was issued to the illustrious Prince on the 4th of Sha'ban, to withdraw his forces from around the fortress, and, deferring its capture till some other period, to take his siege train along with him and set out for Court. . .

'INAYAT KHAN

DEPARTURE OF THE PRINCE BULAND IKBAL DARA SHUKOH FROM LAHORE TO KANDAHAR, AND ORGANISATION OF FORCES WITH ARTILLERY, ETC.

As the Prince Buland Ikbal, after the return of the army from Kandahar, had guaranteed to conquer that territory, and with this view the provinces of Kabul and Multan had been bestowed upon him, His Royal Highness, on reaching the capital, applied himself to the task of making the requisite arrangements for the campaign. In the course of three months and some days that he remained at Lahore, he used such profuse exertions, that what could not have been otherwise accomplished in a year was effected in this short period. Among the siege train was a gun called *Kishwar-kusha* (clime-conquering), and another *Garh-bhanjan* (fort-shattering), each of which carried an iron shot one *man* and eight *sirs* in weight (96 lbs.); and they were worked by the gunners under the direction of Kasim Khan.

There was also another large piece of ordnance that carried a shot of a *man* and sixteen *sirs* (1 cwt.), and was plied under the management of His Royal Highness's *Mir-i atish*, as well as 30,000 cannon-balls, small and great. He also got ready 5,000 *mans* of gunpowder, and 2,500 of lead, measuring by Imperial weight, and 14,000 rockets. Having likewise collected as many grain dealers as were procurable, he made arrangements for the army commissariat, and the safe arrival of supplies. He then despatched a letter to Court, representing that as the moment of starting was fixed for the 23rd of Rabi'u-l awwal, and the preliminary arrangements for the campaign had been completed, if the royal forces appointed to this enterprise received their dismissal, he would set out for Kandahar. A mandate in the auspicious handwriting was therefore issued, directing His Royal Highness to start off at the predetermined moment by way of Multan, on which road provisions and forage were abudant. (*Long details of the siege.*)

TWENTY-SEVENTH YEAR OF THE REIGN, 1063 A.H. (1652-3 A.D.)

Reduction of the Fortress of Bust

Among the stirring incidents that occurred during the siege of Kandahar was the subjugation of the fortress of Bust by the laudable exertions of the servants of the crown, a concise account of which is as follows. . . .

SIEGE OF KANDAHAR RAISED

Ultimately the duration of the siege extended beyond five months, the winter began to set in, all the lead, powder, and cannon-balls were expended, and neither was there any forage left in the meadows, nor provisions with the army. A *farman* likewise was issued to this effect, that as the winter was close at hand, and they had already been long detained in Kandahar, if the reduction of the fortress could not be effected just at once. they might stay if necessary some short time longer; or otherwise return immediately. Rustam Khan, who had been recalled from Bust for the purpose of sharing in the assault, having dismantled that fortress, distributed the provisions among his men, and reached Kandahar with his comrades, bringing all the artillery stores, and property in the *Kar-khana,* that was there, along with him. With an eye therefore to the safety of the property mentioned above, he deemed it expedient to return, and not one of the royalist commanders proposed staying any longer. The Prince Buland Ikbal consequently, on the 15th Zi-l ka'da this year, set out from Kandahar for Hindustan.

TWENTY-EIGHTH YEAR OF THE REIGN, 1064 A.H. (1653-4 A.D.)

Appointment of 'Allami to the task of demolishing the Fort of Chitor, and Chastising the Rana

On the 22nd Zi-l ka'da, at a chosen moment. the

royal departure from the metropolis of Shahjahanabad to the blessed city of Ajmir took place. On the same date, the Emperor despatched 'Allami, with a large number of nobles and *mansabdars* and 1,500 musketeers, amounting altogether to 30,000, for the purpose of hurrying on in that direction, and demolishing the fort of Chitor, which was one of the gifts (*'ataya*) that had been made by this Imperial dynasty. From the time of the late Emperor Jahangir, it had been settled that no one of the Rana's posterity should ever fortify it; but Rana Jagat Singh, the father of Raja Jai Singh, having set about repairing it, had pulled down every part that was damaged, and built it up very strongly anew. He also directed him, if perchance the Rana did not tender his obedience, to overrun his territory with the royal forces, and inflict suitable chastisement on him. The triumphant standards then moved on by the regular marches in the rear of the ever-victorious troops. On the 2nd of Zi-l hijja, when the world-subduing banners were planted at Khalilpur, the Rana's confidential *vakils* waited on the Prince Buland Iqbal, and begged His Royal Highness to act as their intercessor. When, by his mediation, the penitence and humility expressed by the Rana was reported at the threshold of might and majesty, an order was issued that His Royal Highness should send his *Mir-i buyutat* to wait upon the Rana, and deliver the following message, viz., that if, with judicious forethought, he would despatch his eldest son, the *Sahib-i-tika,* to the presence, and a detachment of his people under the command of one of his relatives were stationed in the Dakhin, the same as formerly, to be employed in the royal service, he should be left in security, or otherwise he should be overhelmed in adversity.

As the Rana had again in these days humbly forwarded an address to the Prince Buland Ikbal, requesting him to send his *diwan,* in order that he might start off his sons to Court in company with that indivudal, His Royal Highness obtained permission from the Imperial thereshold, and despatched Shaikh 'Abdu-l Karim, his own *diwan,* to the Rana. . . .

The exploits of the army that accompanied 'Allami were as follows. On his arriving within twelve *kos* of Chitor, which is the frontier of the Rana's territory, inasmuch as the latter's negotiations had not yet been satisfactorily terminated, he commenced plundering and devasting, and depasturing his cattle on the crops. On the 5th of Zi-l hijja, this year, having reached the environs of Chitor, he directed working parties with pickaxes and spades to overthrow that powerful stronghold. Accordingly, in the course of fourteen or fifteen days, they laid its towers and battlements in ruins, and having dug up and subverted both the old and the new walls, levelled the whole to the ground. The Rana having awoke from his sleep of heedlessness at the advent of the prosperous banners at Ajmir, the irresistible force of the royal arms, the dispersion of the peasantry, and the ruin of his territory, sent off a letter containing the humblest apologies to Court, along with his eldest son, who was in his sixth year, and a number of his principal retainers, in company with Shaikh 'Abdu-l Karim, the Prince Buland Ikbal's Mir-i *buyutat.* A *farman* was then issued to Jamdatu-l Mulk ('Allami), that since the fort had been demolished, and the Rana had sent off his son to Court, the pen of forgiveness had been drawn through the register of his delinquencies at the Prince Buland Ikbal's solicitation, and that he would set out himself with the whole of the victorious army to the royal presence.

MARKS OF DISTINCTION BESTOWED ON PRINCE DARA SHUKOH

On the 8th of Rabi'us sani this year, being the expiration of the sixty-fifth lunar year of His Majesty's age, a festival was celebrated with exceeding splendour, and was attended with the usual ceremonies. In this sublime assembly the Emperor kindly conferred on the

Prince Buland Ikbal a handsome *khil'at* with a gold-embroidered vest, studded with valuable diamonds round the collar; on both sleeves, and the skirts, pearls had been sewn, and it was worth 50,000 rupees; also a *sarband* composed of a single ruby of the purest water, and two magnificent pearls, of the value of a *lac* and 70,000 rupees, and a donation of thirty *lacs* besides. He also distinguished His Royal Highness by the lofty title of Shah Buland Ikbal, which had been applied exclusively to himself during his late Majesty's reign; and since in the days of Princehood a chair had been placed at that Emperor's suggestion opposite to the throne for him to sit on, he now in like manner directed His Royal Highness to seat himself on a golden chair, that had been placed near the sublime throne.

TWENTY-NINTH YEAR OF THE REIGN, 1065 A.H. (1654-5 A.D.)

Campaign in Sirmor

Among the incidents of the past year, the appointment and despatch of Khalilu-lla Khan during the return from Ajmir, with 8000 men, for the purpose of cocercing the Zamindar of Srinagar, and capturing the Dun. have been already detailed by the historic pen. The particulars of his advance and return are as follows. When the Khan in question set out with the royal forces, the Zamindar of Sirmor, who had never felt disposed to ally himself with the servants of the crown, came under the guidance of good fortune and joined them. He was then rendered conspicous among his compeers by the promulgation of an edict from the threshold of empire and sovereignty. investing him with the title of Raja Sabhak Prakas.

Sirmor is a mountainous tract to the north of the new metropolis, measuring thirty *kos* in length. and twenty-five in breadth, in which ice-houses had been established for His Majesty's private use; whence, form the beginning of the month Isfandiar (February) till the end of Mihr

(September), an abundant supply of ice was constantly reaching the metropolis during the time that the royal standards were planted there. From these emporia porters used to carry loads of snow and ice on their backs as far as Dhamras, the name of a place situated on the bank of the river Jumna at a distance of sixteen *kos*, but the road to which is extremely difficult. There it was packed in boxes, and sent down the stream on rafts to Daryapur, one of the dependencies of *pargana* Khizrabad, which is also sixteen *kos* off from Dhamras. From that point it was transported to the metropolis on board of boats in the course of three days and nights.

Khalilu-lla Khan, in company with the aforesaid Raja and some other *zamindars* of those parts, having reached the Dun, which is a strip of country lying outside of Srinagar, twenty *kos* long and five broad, one extremity of its length being bounded by the river Jumna, and the other by the Ganges, which possesses many flourishing towns in various quarters, laid the foundation of a field-work close to Kilaghar, and completed it in the course of a week. He then deputed one of the *mansabdars* to keep guard there with 200 matchlockmen, and set out in advance with the whole of his comrades. On reaching Bahadur Khanpur, which is a place belonging to the Dun, and lies between the rivers Jumna and Ganges, in consequence of the peasantry that dwelt in that neighbourhood having taken refuge in the hills and forests and defiles, and obstinately refusing to return, he despatched the ever-triumphant troops from every side to coerce them, who succeeded in inflicting suitable chastisement. A number of the rebels therefore fell by the sword of vengeance, and many more were taken prisoners; after which the remainder tendered their allegiance, and innumerable herds of cattle fell into the hands of the solidiery. Here, likewise, he threw up a fortified post, and left a confidential person with some *mansabdars*, and 500 infantry and matchlockmen, to garrison it, so that the passage of travellers to and fro might remain uninterrupted. Having then set out himself from thence, he approached the town of Basantpur, which is also a dependency of the Dun, and halted half-way up the hill. Opposite the above town, he constructed another redoubt, in which he posted one of the *mansabdars* with 250 infantry matchlockmen. From thence he moved to Sahijpur, a place abounding in streams and fountains, and clothed with flowers and verdure; where he erected a fort on the top of an embankment, measuring 1,000 yards in circumference, and fifteen in height, that had in former times been crowned by a stronghold, inasmuch as some traces of the ancient works were still visible; and he deputed a trusty individual to hold the post, backed by 250 musketeers. On reaching the banks of the Ganges, after crossing which one enters the hill-country, he sent a detachment with the royal artillery to the other side of the stream, with a view to their taking possession of the *thana* of Chandi, which is one of the dependencies of Srinagar, but lies outside the Dun of Kilaghar.

Meanwhile, Bahadur Chand, Zamindar of Kumayun (Kumaon), under the guidance of a fortunate destiny, espoused the royal cause, and came and joined the above-mentioned Khan. As soon as this fact was conveyed to the Imperial ear, the repository of all good, through the representations of Khalilu-lla Khan, a conciliatory *farman* and a *khil'at* set with jewels were forwarded to him. As the season for prosecuting military operations in that region and the fitting period for an invasion of the hill-country had passed away, the rains being now at hand, and the Dun having been taken possession of, a mandate was issued to Khalilu-lla Khan, to defer the campaign in the hills for the present: and after delivering up the Dun to Chatur Bhuj, who had expressed an ardent desire for it, and confiding the *thana* of Chandi to Nagar Das, the chief of Hardwar, to set out for Court. The Khan accordingly, having set his mind at rest by fulfilling these instructions, started for the presence.

MIR JUMLA SEEKS PROTECTION

Another incident was the flying for refuge of Mir Muhammad Sa'id Ardastani, surnamed Mir Jumla,[5] to the Court, the asylum of mankind, an account of which event is as follows. The above individual, in whose hands was the entire administration of Kutbu-l Mulk's kingdom, had, after a severe struggle with the Karnatikis, brought under subjection, in addition to a powerful fort, a tract of country measuring 150 *kos* in length, and twenty or thirty in breadth, and yielding a revenue of forty *lacs* of rupees. It also contained mines teeming with diamonds, and no one of Kutbu-l Mulk's ancestors had ever been able to gain possession of any portion of it. Having destroyed several strong forts built by the Karnatikis, he had brought this country into his power; and in spite of long-standing usages, he had collected a considerable force, so that he had 5,000 horse in his service. For these reasons, a faction who were at enmity with him caused Kutbu-l Mulk to be displeased with him, and strove to effect his ruin. He had been active in perfoming such meritorious services, and after contending against the *zamindars* of the Karnatik, had subdued so fine a territory, but he did not gain the object he sought; but, on the contrary, reaped disappointment. So, using Prince Mahammad Aurangzeb Bahadur as an intercessor, he sought refuge at the Court, the asylum of the world. After this circumstance had been disclosed to the world-adorning understanding through the representations of the illustrious Prince, a handsome *khil'at* was forwarded to him by the hand of one of the courtiers in the middle of this month.

[5](*Afterwards entitled Mu'azzam Khan.*)

together with an indulgent *farman* sanctioning the bestowal of a *mansab* of 5000 on him, and one of 2,000 on his son, Mir Muhammad Amin; as well as a mandate accompanied by a superb dress of honour for Kutbu-l Mulk, regarding the not prohibiting him and his relations from coming.

ACCOUNT OF PRINCE MUHAMMAD AURANGZEB'S MARCH TO GOLKONDA[6]

Among the important events that took place towards the close of this year was the march of the ever-successful Prince Muhammad Aurangzeb Bahadur to the territory of Golkonda, for the sake of coercing Kutbu-l Mulk, his exaction of a superb tributary offering on behalf of His Majesty's private exchequer, and his uniting in marriage of the latter's daughter with his own eldest son, Muhammad Sultan, an abridged narrative of which is as follows. When Mir Jumla sought to ally himself to the Imperial throne, Kutbu-l Mulk, the instant he gained intelligence of the matter, imprisoned Mir Jumla's son, Mir Muhammad Amin, together with his connexions, and having confiscated whatever he possessed, both in livestock and goods, forwarded him and his relatives to Golkonda. This circumstance having soon reached the ear of the fortunate Prince, through the intervention of news-writers, His Royal Highness despatched a quiet letter to Kutbu-l Mulk regarding the release of the prisoners, and the restoration of Mir Muhammad Amin's goods and chattels. Having likewise reported the state of the case to the Imperial presence, he solicited authority, that in case Kutbu-l Mulk persisted in keeping Mir Jumla's son in confinement, he might be permitted to march

[6]*(Both Muhammad Waris and Muhammad Salih agree in placing these affairs of Golkonda in the thirtieth year of the reign.)*

against him in person, and endeavour to liberate the captives; as supineness in restoring to arms would be a source of additional lethargy to the opulent lords of the Dakhin. On the receipt of his report, a *farman* was likewise forwarded with the utmost expedition to Kutbu-l Mulk, by the hands of some mace-bearers, respecting the surrender of Mir Jumla's son along with his relatives, and the infliction of the consequences of disobedience. A mandate was also addressed to the victorious Prince, instructing him to set out for his destination with the triumphant troops; and the ever-obeyed commands were issued to the governor of Malwa, and the *mansabdars* serving in that province, to proceed and join His Royal Highness as quickly as possible.

In short, as Kutbu-l Mulk, under the influence of the fumes of arrogance, would not heed the contents of the letter, the Prince despatched his eldest son, Muhammad Sultan, thither on the 8th of Rabi'u-l awwal this year, along with a host of nobles and *mansabdars* and his own followers. It was further determined that the army that was returning from Deogarh should halt in that vicinity, and unite itself to the illustrious Sultan; and that he himself should set out afterwards in the course of another month. About this time, the *mansabdars* in whose charge the *khil'ats* and *farmans* had been despatched for Kutbu-l Mulk and Mir Jumla from the brilliant presence, as has been related in its proper place, came and waited on that ward of the divine vigilance. Although it was the realm-subduing Prince's opinion that Kutbu-l Mulk would release Mir Jumla's son from confinement previous to the arrival of Muhammad Sultan, "the tender sapling in the garden of prosperity and success," at the frontier of the Golkonda territory, and that the campaign would not consequently be prolonged to any great extent, yet Kutbu-l Mulk, from excessive negligence and extreme pride. had not the good sense to adopt this measure, and hold the *farman* in dread and fear. After the last communication the Prince gave orders,[7] directing Muhammad Sultan to enter his territory with the Imperial troops. On receiving the above *farman* with the alarming intelligence of Muhammad Sultan's approach at the head of the royal forces, Kutbu-l Mulk awake from his deep sleep, of arrogance and conceit, and sent off Mir Jumla's son, along with his mother and connexions. He also forwarded a letter to Court, intimating this fact, and avowing his fealty and subservience, in charge of the mace-bearers who had brought the *farman*. Mir Jumla's son having joined Muhammad Sultan twelve *kos* from Haidarabad, reposed in the cradle of peace and safety. Nevertheless as Kutbu-l Mulk, with grasping avarice, still retained the goods and property belonging to Mir Jumla and his son, and would not deliver them up, the illustrious Sultan set out for the city of Haidarabad. Kutbu-l Mulk, on learning this news, started off his children to Golkonda, which is situated at a distance of three *kos* from Haidarabad, and where owing to the impregnability of the position, he was in the habit of depositing his secret hoards of treasure; and he followed them shortly after himself. Whatever gems and jewelry, gold and silver articles, and cash he possessed, he likewise removed to the fort of Golkonda; and other property, such as various kinds of carpets, porcelain, etc., he made over to the chief of his confidential servants, and deputed him to contend with the royal forces.

Next morning, corresponding to the 5th of Rabi'u-s sani this year, when Muhammad Sultan, having arrived at the environs of Haidarabad, was just about to encamp on the banks of the Husain Sajar lake, one of Kutbu-l Mulk's confidential retainers came and waited on him with a casket full of jewels that his master had

[7] *(The text here is vague and of doubtful meaning.)*

forwarded by his hands. Meanwhile, Kutbu-l Mulk's forces made their appearance, and assumed a menacing attitude; but the ever-triumphant troops, having engaged in the deadly strife from right and left, enveloped the enemy with speed and promptitude in the midst of a galling fire, and by the aid of His Majesty's daily-increasing good fortune, having gained the superiority, chased the routed fugitives up to the city walls. Many of the enemy were accordingly killed and wounded, and the survivors, from dread of the royalists' assaults, did not stay within the city walls, but fled into the fort. In short, as such an audacious act had been perpetrated by Kutbu-l Mulk, and the bearer of the casket of jewels was indicated as the originator of this hostile movement, Muhammad Sultan gave the order for his execution.

ARRIVAL OF MUHAMMAD SULTAN AT GOLKONDA, AND SUBJUGATION OF HAIDARABAD

On the morrow, Muhammad Sultan took possession of the city of Haidarabad, and having encamped outside the walls, prohibited the soldiery from entering it, for fear of having Kutbu-l Mulk's property plundered, and the effects of the inhabitants carried off. He also despatched a confidential servant of his noble father to conciliate the residents of that city, so as to dissuade them from dispersing, and to endeavour to protect their wealth and property. This day Kutbu-l Mulk sent 200 more caskets full of gems and jewelled trinkets, two elephants with silver housings, and four horses with gold trappings, to the Sultan; and that fruitful plant of the gardens of prosperity and good fortune detained the bearer of these articles in his camp, as a hostage for the restoration of Mir Jumla's goods, which Kutbu-l Mulk still persisted in withholding. Five or six days afterwards, he sent eleven elephants, sixty horses, and other things belonging to Mir Jumla; and though, apparently having entered into amicable relations, he used to send numbers of people to Muhammad Sultan, and make professions of loyal obedience, yet he continued strengthening his fortifications, using tremendous exertions to complete the requisite preparations for standing a siege, and forwarded repeated letters to 'Adil Khan by the hands of trusty individuals soliciting aid.

ARRIVAL OF THE FORTUNATE PRINCE AT GOLKONDA

The particulars regarding the ever-triumphant Prince's retinue are as follows. His Royal Highness having reached Golkonda from Aurangabad in eighteen days, pitched his camp on the 20th of the aforesaid Rabi'u-s sani a *kos* from the fort. He then went oft the road for the purpose of marking out the intrenchments, and reconnoitring the defences of the place, and having gained intelligence of Kutbu-l Mulk's approach, commanded Muhammad Sultan to take post on the left-hand side with his force. At this juncture, five or six thousand cavalry and ten or twelve thousand infantry came opposite to the army, and killed the flame of war by discharging rockets and matchlocks, whilst the garrison likewise fired off numerous cannons and rockets, from the top of the ramparts. The lion-hearted Prince, however, with his habitual intrepidity, allowed no apprehensions to enter his mind, but urged on his riding elephant to the front; and the heroes of the arena of strife, having charged at full gallop in successive squadrons, and sapped the foundations of their foolish opponents' stability by their irresistible assaults, victory declared in favour of the servants of the crown. The ever-triumphant Prince, after returning to camp, crowned with glory and success, despatched the royalists to besiege the fort, and the prosecution of the attack against each front was committed to the vigilant superintendence of some trusty individual.

In short, the friends of Government began constructing intrenchments, and carrying forward the approaches; and as Kutbu-l Mulk, from weakness of intellect, had been guilty of such highly improper behaviour, notwithstanding that he had again sent four more caskets of gems, three elephants with silver housings, and five horses with gold and silver trappings, in charge of an intimate friend, begging that he might be allowed to send his mother to wait upon His Royal Highness, for the purpose of asking pardon for his offences; the Prince, in token of his deep displeasure, would not listen to his request, nor grant his messenger an audience, but exhorted the besiegers to lavish still greater exertions in carrying on the attack with gallantry and vigour. After two or three days had elapsed in this manner, a vast force of the Kutbu-l Mulkis made their appearance on the northern side of fort, and were about to pour down upon the intrenchment of Mirza Khan, who was engaged in the defence of that quarter; when the latter, becoming aware of their hostile intention, made an application for reinforcements. The renowned and successful Prince immediately despatched some nobles with his own artillery to his support; and these reinforcements having arrived at full speed, took part at once in the affray. Under the magic influence of His Majesty's never-failing good fortune, the enemy took to flight; whereupon the ever-triumphant troops began putting the miscreants to the sword, and allowed hardly any of them to escape death or captivity. After chasing the vain wretches as far as the fort, they brought the prisoners, along with an elephant that had fallen into their hands, into His Royal Highness's presence.

On this date a trusty person was deputed to go and fetch Mir Jumla; and as it reached the Prince's auspicious ear that about six or seven thousand cavalry and nearly 20,000 infantry of Kutbu-l Mulk, consisting principally of matchlockmen, who had been repeatedly defeated and dispersed in the battles mentioned above, had collected together on the southern face of the fort, and were standing prepared for action, the illustrious

Prince mounted and set out in person to exterminate the doomed wretches. As soon as he drew near, the miscreants had the fool-hardiness to advance, and standing on the brink of a ravine that ran between them, fanned the flame of strife into a blaze by the discharge of matchlocks and rockets; whilst from the battlements of the fort also, cannons, guns, and rockets beyond number, played upon him incessantly. The devoted heroes, however, drawing the shield of divine Providence over their heads, pushed rapidly across the ravine; and a detachment of their vanguard, by the most spirited efforts, drove the villains two or three times to the foot of the ramparts, hurling many of them into the dust of destruction, and capturing a number more. Several of the servants of the Crown perished in this conflict, and others were adorned with the cosmetic of wounds; whilst a number of the Prince's retainers also were either killed or wounded. His Royal Highness, deeming an additional force necessary for this quarter, stationed one there, and having taken possession of the commanding points, and appointed a party of matchlockmen to guard them, returned at night from the field of battle to his own tents.

Next day, at Muhammad Sultan's solicitation, he gave Kutbu-l Mulk's son-in-law permission to pay his respects, who had come two days before with some petitions and a slight tributary offering, but had not gained admittance. Having refused the jewelry that the latter had brought for him, he deferred its acceptance till the conclusion of negotiations. About this time Shayista Khan joined the army with the nobles of Malwa, whereupon the Prince altered the previous position of the trenches, and directed that they should throw up four, opposite each front of the fortifications. In these very days, too, an Imperial edict arrived, intimating the despatch of a handsome *khil'at,* and a jewelled dagger with *phul-katar*, for the illustrious Prince, and a present of a fine dress of honour, and a *mansab* of 7,000, with 2,000 horse, for Muhammad Sultan, as well as a benevolent *farman* to Kutbu-l Mulk's address, granting him a free pardon. By the untiring efforts of the servants of the Crown, however, affairs had come to such a pass, that Kutbu-l Mulk was all but annihilated, and every day a number of his followers used to turn the countenance of hope towards this prosperous threshold, and attain the honour of paying their respects. Alarmed at the irresistible superiority of the royal troops, moreover, he had sent two of his confidential servants with a tributary offering, and tendered his allegiance, consenting to pay all the stipulated tribute, due for several years up to Isfandiar of the 29th year of this reign, and begging that the amount of that for the present twelvemonth might be settled in addition to the former. The subject of his daughter's marriage with Muhammad Sultan had likewise been broached; and the illustrious Prince, consequently, deeming it inexpedient to forward him the warrant of pardon just now, kept it to himself. After a lapse of two or three days, Kutbu-l Mulk despatched, agreeably to orders, ten elephants and some jewelry, as an instalment of the tribute in arrears, together with two more elephants and other articles belonging to Mir Jumla's son. For the noble Muhammad Sultan, too, he sent a letter congratulating him on his *mansab,* two elephants, one of which bore silver housings, and a horse with gold saddle and jewelled trappings. The Prince then directed that they should mount two heavy guns that had been brought from fort Usa, on the top of a mound situated in Katalabi Khan's intrenchment, and point them against the fortress.

As Kutbu-l Mulk had repeatedly begged permission to send his mother for the purpose of asking pardon for his offences, and solicited a safe conduct, it was ordered that Muhammad Sultan and Shayista Khan should despatch the customary passport. As soon as he received that warrant and security, he sent off his mother in the hope of gaining his other objects. Accordingly, on the 22nd of Jumada-l awwal, several of His Royal Highness's intimate companions went out, at his suggestion, to meet her, and brought her from the road to Shayista Khan's camp. The latter, having treated her with the deepest respect and attention, conducted her next day, agreeably to orders, into the illustrious presence; where she enjoyed an interview with Muhammad Sultan, and presented two horses. As Muhammad Sultan represented that she was anxious to be admitted to a personal audience, in order to detail her propositions, the Prince summoned her into his presence. That chaste matron then presented a thousand gold *mohurs* as *nisar* to His Royal Highness as well as.

That ward of divine providence affirmed in reply, that Kutub-l Mulk must pay down a *kror* of rupees in cash, jewelry, elephants, etc., and she having consented to obey this mandate, returned to the fortress for the purpose of collecting the above sum.

As a vast number of Kutbu-l Mulk's partisans, under the command of his *kotwal,* who had no intimation as yet of the armistice, had collected together about two *kos* from the fortress with hostile intentions, the Prince despatched several nobles and *mansabdars,* with 200 mounted musketeers, and 500 cavalry out of Shayista Khan's retainers, amounting altogether to 6,000 horse, and a host of matchlockmen, to coerce them. The royal troops repaired with the utmost celerity to the menaced point, and encamped that day close to the enemy's position. On the succeeding one, the miscreants sent off their heavy baggage and property to a distance, and having formed up in line themselves, stood prepared for action. Although the royalists several times drove them off and dispersed them, yet the shameless wretches kept constantly rallying and renewing their assaults, in which they suffered numerous casualties, until night supervened: when the ill-fated villains, being incapable of further resistance, took to a precipitate flight. A few out of the victorious army were also killed and wounded; and the ever-successful troops, after spending the night on the ground where the enemy's tents had stood, returned in triumph on the morrow.

MIR JUMLA'S COMING TO WAIT UPON THE PRINCE MUHAMMAD AURANGZEB BAHADUR

At this time, the news of Mir Jumla's arrival in the vicinity of Golkonda was made known; so, the Prince forward to him the *farman* and *Khil'at* that had come for him from Court, by the hands of the bearer of it. The latter having been apprised of the fact. came out to meet the messenger, from his camp, which was pitched four *kos* the other side of the Husain Sagar lake, and after observing the usual marks of respect, received the *farman* and *khil'at* from him on the banks of the above named lake. As two days were wanting to the time fixed for his introduction to the victorious Prince, he returned for the present to his own camp. On the appointed day, the Prince sent out some nobles to fetch him, and he having set out with great pomp and splendour, enjoyed at a chosen moment the honour of paying his respects, and presented 3.000 *Ibrahimis* as *nisar*. That descendant of nobles was recompensed from the munificent threshold by the receipt of a superb dress of honour, a jewelled *tarrah* and dagger, two horses, one with a gold. the other with a silver saddle, and an elephant with silver housings, accompanied by a female one; and obtained permission to be seated in the presence. As peace had now been established on a firm basis, the fortunate and successful Prince evacuated the trenches encircling the fortress, on the last day of the aforesaid month, and summoned the party engaged in the siege to his presence.

'INAYAT KHAN

THIRTIETH YEAR OF THE REIGN, 1066 A.H. (1655-6 A.D.)
PAINFUL DEATH OF SA'DU-LLA KHAN

On the 22nd Jumada-s sani 'Allami Sa'du-lla Khan, conformably to the sacred text, "When your time of death has arrived, see that ye defer not a moment, nor procrastinate," returned the response of *Labaika* to the herald of God, and migrated from this transitory sphere to the realms of immortality. For nearly four months he had been labouring under a severe and painful attack of cholic; during the first two months of which period, when he was not confined to his bed, he used to attend daily in the auspicious presence, and uttered no exclamation of pain. In fact, he was then trying to dispel the disease by attending to Takarrub Khan's medical treatment; but after he became confined to his house from the acute agony he was suffering, the matter was disclosed to the royal ear; whereupon the skilful physicians in attendance at the foot of the sublime throne were commanded to effect his cure. As his appointed time of death, however, had come, all their remedies produced no effect, and the disease gradually gaining ground, put an end to his sufferings. The monarch, the appreciator of worth, expressed intense regret at the demise of that deserving object of kindness and consideration, and showered favours on his children and all his connexions.

MARRIAGE OF MUHAMMAD SULTAN WITH KUTBU-L MULK'S DAUGHTER

The sequel to the narrative of Golkonda affairs is as follows. As the moment for the celebration of Muhammad Sultan's nuptials had been fixed for the morning of the 18th of Jumada-s sani in this happy-omened year, Prince Muhammad Aurangzeb Bahadur sent his *diwan,* Muhammad Tahir, one day previously to Kutbu-l Mulk, together with the ecclesiastics, and forwarded a *khil'at*. Next day, the marriage service was read in a fortunate moment, and the hymeneal rites were duly observed.

After a week's interval, the illustrious Prince again despatched his own *diwan* and the royal *bakhshi* into the fortress, with a view to fetching that chaste and fortunate damsel; and commanded several nobles to wait outside the fortifications, and accompany her from thence. These obedient vassals accordingly acted in conformity with his injunctions, and conducted her along with Kutbu-l Mulk's mother, who had accompanied her, to a pavilion that had been erected near His Royal Highness's. Kutbu-l Mulk sent about ten *lacs* of rupees in gems and other articles by way of dowry. Next day the Prince forwarded the *farman* and a superb *khil'at* the delivery of which he had deferred, as has been alluded to in its proper place, to Kutbu-l Mulk, who went out to meet them, and received them with the deepest reverence.

(*Return of Prince Muhammad 'Aurangzeb from Golkonda, investiture of Mir Jumla with the title of Mu'azzam Khan, and bestowal of that of Khan-jahan on Shayista Khan.*)

APPOINTMENT OF PRINCE MUHAMMAD AURANGZEB TO CONDUCT THE CAMPAIGN OF BIJAPUR, AND DISMISSAL OF MU'AZZAM KHAN (MIR JUMLA), ETC., FROM THE PRESENCE

Among the events of this year was the appointment of the victorious Prince Aurangzeb Bahadur to conduct the campaign of Bijapur, and the dismissal of Mu'azzam Khan aid the other nobles and *mansabdars* from the sublime presence to share in the above campaign; a concise version of which is as follows. As it had been reported at the threshold of royalty, through the representations of the above-named Prince, that 'Adil Khan had bid adieu to existence by a natural death, and his servants had constituted Majhul Illahi his successor, who professed to be his offspring, it was ordered, on the 18th of Safar, that His Royal Highness should hasten thither with the Dakhin forces, and bring the campaign to a conclusion, in such a way as he should deem expedient. An ever-obeyed mandate was also issued to Khan-Jahan, to repair expeditiously to Daulatabad, and remain in that city until the ever-successful Prince's return. Jamdatu-l Mulk Mu'azzam Khan, Shah Nawaz Khan Safvi, Mahabat Khan, Nijabat Khan, Raja Rai Singh, and a number of more nobles and *mansabdars,* whose total strength amounted to 20,000 horse, were appointed to serve under that ward of divine providence; some being despatched from the auspicious presence, and others from their respective homes and *jagirs,* along with a great many musketeers both horse and foot, and rocket-men. Among those who received their dismissal from the presence, Jamdatu-l Mulk was presented with a handsome *khil'at,* etc. . .

As Mu'azzam Khan had reported that he had sent several led horses, adorned with diamonds, rubies, and precious stones, and some other articles, that he had taken from the *Zamindar* of the Karnatik, to 'Adil Khan, the Shah Buland Ikbal despatched by the hands of two confidential slaves a mandate, agreeably to orders. to the latter, respecting the forwarding of the aforesaid articles. As 'Adil Khan, however, departed this life very shortly after the receipt of the mandate, his servants forwarded to Court four out of the whole number of led horses, together with an epistle from his successor, in charge of the above-mentioned slaves. They were accordingly presented on the 1st of Rabi'u-s sani this year, and their value was almost a *lac* of rupees.

BADSHAH-NAMA
OF
MUHAMMAD WARIS

This work is also called *Shah Jahan-nama*. It is the completion of the *Badshah-nama* of 'Abdu-l Hamid by his pupil and assistant Muhammad Waris, who was appointed to carry on the work when his friend and master had become incapacitated by age. It embraces the last ten years of Shah Jahan's reign, from the beginning of the twenty-first to the thirtieth year, in which his actual reign closed. The work was submitted for revision to 'Alau-l Mulk Tuni, entitled Fazil Khan. who became *wazir* in Aurangzeb's days and the part of the work subsequent to the death of 'Allami Sa'du-lla Khan was written by Fazil Khan, under the command of the Emperor himself. Little is known of Muhammad Waris, but the author of the Ma-asir-i 'Alamgiri records that "On the 10th Rabi'u-l awwal, 1091 (1680 A.D.)., Waris Khan, news reader, the graceful author of the third volume of the *Badshah-nama,* was killed by a blow of a pen-knife from a mad student, whom he had taken under his protection, and who used to sleep at night near his patron."

The work is composed in a style similar to that of 'Abdu-l Hamid, and is of considerable length. It closes with a list of the *shaikhs,* learned men and poets who flourished during its decade.

The history of this period of Shah Jahan's reign has been so fully supplied by the Extracts from the *Shah Jahan-nama* of 'Inayat Khan, that only one short Extract has been taken from this work.

Sir H. M. Elliot's MS. is a poor one. It is an 8vo., twelve inches by six and a half, and contains 357 leaves, of nineteen lines to the page. There is a copy in the

F. 9.

MUHAMMAD WARIS

British Museum, and one in the Library of the Royal Asiatic Society.

EXTRACT

Twenty-Second Year of the Reign

When the Emperor set off from Shahjahanabad to chastise the Persians, it was his intention to march on and make no stay until he reached Kabul. . . But afterwards it appeared clear to his far-reaching judgment, that it was very improbable that the Shah of Persia would enter upon a campaign in the winter season, when grain and forage are very difficult to procure in that country (of Kandahar). The Emperor's counsellors also represented that the Shah of Persia had resolved upon this evil enterprise in that infatuation which arises from youth and inexperience. During the winter he would be busy making preparations in Khurasan, and in the spring he would commence operations. In this way the late Shah 'Abbas came up against Kandahar in the reign of the Emperor Jahangir. The severe cold and the heavy snow and rain, together with scarcity of provender for the horses, would be sources of great suffering to the Imperial army; so under all circumstances it was desirable to postpone the march until the Nau-roz. . . So it was resolved to wait the arrival of news from Kandahar. On the 12th Muharram a despatch arrived from the commandant of the fortress, to the effect that on the 10th Zil-hijja the Shah of Persia had invested the fortress, his evident object being to accomplish this, the first enterprise of his reign, before the spring, when the roads would be open for the advance of the Imperial army.

'AMAL-I SALIH
OF
MUHAMMAD SALIH KAMBU

(This, like the other histories of the reign of Shah Jahan, is sometimes called *Shah Jahan-nama*. It is a history of the reign of that Emperor from his birth to his death in 1076 A.H. (1665 A.D.).

Muhammad Salih was a fine scribe, so there can be little doubt that he is the Muhammad Salih he himself mentions in his list of the noted caligraphists of his time. Mir Muhammad Salih and Mir Muhammad Muman were, he says, sons of Mir 'Abdu-lla, *Mushkin kalam,* whose title shows him to have also been a fine writer. Muhammad Salih was known as a poet by the Persian title *Kashfi* and the Hindi *Subhan*. Both brothers were not only fine writers, but accomplished Hindi singers. In the list of *mansabdars*, Muhammad Salih is put down as commander of five hundred.

The *'Amal-i Salih* is a valuable history, and has a good reputation in the East. It is not so long as the *Badshah-nama* of 'Abdu-l Hamid and Muhammad Waris, and it does not enter into the same petty details. The latter part of it, devoted to the life of Shah Jhan after his deposition, is very brief, and notices only the tragic deaths of his sons and his own peaceful decease. The style is polished, and often highly wrought and rhetorical. At the end of the work the author has added biographical notices of the *saiyids, shaikhs,* learned men, physicians, poets, and fine writers who were contemporary with Shah Jahan. Also a list of princes, nobles, and commanders, arranged according to their respective ranks. A borrowed MS., belonging to a native gentleman, is a folio 13 in × 9, containing about 1,000 to 1,200 pages).

MUHAMMAD SALIH KAMBU

EXTRACTS

THIRTY-FIRST YEAR OF THE REIGN

Death of 'Ali Mardan Khan

Amiru-l Umara 'Ali Mardan Khan, being ill with dysentery, started for Kashmir, the air of which country suited his constitution, but he died on his way on the 12th Rajab. . . . His sons, Ibrahim Khan and the others, brought his corpse to Lahore, and buried it in the tomb of his mother. He was a noble of the highest dignity; he held a *mansab* of 7,000 with 7,000 horse, 5,000 *do-aspas* and *sih-aspas*. He had an *in'am* of one *kror* of *dams*. Altogether his emoluments amounted to thirty *lacs* of rupees. His death caused the Emperor great grief.

Mu'azzam Khan Joins Aurangzeb. Capture of several fortresses belonging to Bijapur. Defeat of 'Adil Khan's army

Mu'azzam Khan departed from Court, and marched with the army under his command to Prince Aurangzeb, whom he joined on the 12th Rabi'u-s sani. On the same day the Prince, making no delay, marched on his enterprise with all the Imperial forces and his own followers In the course of fourteen days he reached Chandor. There he left Wali Mahaldar Khan with a force of matchlockmen, etc., to keep open the communications and provide supplies. Next day he encamped under the fort of Bidar. This fortress was held by Sidi Marjan, an old servant of Ibrahim 'Adil Khan. He had been commander of the fortress for thirty years, and had kept it fully armed and ready. He had under him nearly 1,000 horse and 4,000 infantry, consisting of musketeers, rocketmen and gunners. The bastions and walls and works were carefully looked after, and he made every preparation for sustaining a siege. As soon as Prince Aurangzeb reached the place, he resolved to reduced it. This strong fortress was 4,500 yards (*dara* in circucumference, and twelve yards high; and it had three deep ditches twenty-five yards (*gaz*) wide, and fifteen yards deep cut in the stone. The Prince went out with Mu'azzam Khan and reconnoitred the fort on all sides. He settled the places for the lines of approach, and named the forces which were to maintain them. Notwithstanding the heavy fire kept up from the bastions and the citadel, in the course of ten days Mu'azzam Khan and the other brave commanders pushed their guns up to the very edge of the ditch and began to fill it up. Several times the garrison sallied forth and made fierce attacks upon the trenches, but each time they were driven back with a great loss in killed and wounded. The besiegers by the fire of their guns destroyed two bastions and battered down the battlements of the wall.

On the 23rd Jumada-s sani, in the thirty-first year of the reign, Muhammad Murad, with a body of musketeers and other forces, sallied from his trenches to make the assault. As soon as he reached the bastion opposite the trench of Mu'azzam Khan, he planted scaling ladders in several places, and ascended the wall. Marjan, the commandant, had dug a great hole in the rear of this bastion, and had filled it with gunpowder, rockets and grenades (*hukka*). With his eight sons and all his personal followers he stood near this bastion, and with the greatest courage and determination endeavoured to resist the assault. Just then, through the good fortune which at all times attends the royal arms, ... a rocket directed against the besiegers fell into the above-mentioned hole, and ignited the gunpowder. A tremendous explosion followed, which destroyed many of the enemy. Sidi Marjan and two of his sons were severely burnt. Those who escaped the explosion bore him and his sons back into the citadel. The brave assailants took advantage of this accident, and pouring into the fortress on all sides, they killed or bore down all who resisted, and raised the flag of victory. . . . The commandant of the fortress, with great humility, sued for quarter, and as he was mortally wounded and unable to move, he sent his sons with the keys of the fortress. They were graciously received by the Prince, who presented them with *khil'ats,* and promised them the Imperial favour. On the day after the giving up the keys, the Prince entered the city, and proceeding to a mosque which had been built two hundred years before, in the reign of the Bahmani Sultans, he caused the *khutba* to be read in the name of the Emperor. . . This strong fortress was thus taken in twenty-seven days. Twelve *lacs* of rupees in money, and eight *lacs* of rupees in lead, gunpowder, stores, and other munitions of a fortress, were obtained, besides two hundred and thirty guns.

Bidar is a pleasant, well-built city, and stands on the borders of Telingana. It is related in the histories of Hindustan, that Bidar was the seat of government of the Rais of the Dakhin, and that the Rais of the Karnatik, Mahratta (country), and Telingana were subject to the Rai of Bidar. Daman, the beloved of King Nala of Malwa, whose story Shaikh Faizi has told in the poem entitled *Nal o Daman,* was daughter of Bhim Sen, the *marzban* of Bidar. Sultan Muhammad, son of Sultan Tughlik, first subdued the place. After that, it passed into the hands of the Bahamanis, and subsequently into the possession of the Kings of Bijapur. By the favour of God, it now forms part of the Imperial dominions.

Intelligence reached the Prince that large bodies of the forces of 'Adil Khan were collecting at Kulbarga, and preparing for war. He consequently sent Mahabat Khan with fifteen thousand well-mounted veteran cavalry to chastise these forces, and not to leave one trace of cultivation in that country. Every building and habitation was to be thrown down, and the land was to be made a dwelling for the owls and kites. The Khan had not got far from Bidar, when, in the middle of the

'AMAL-I SALIH

next day, two thousand of the enemy's horse, at about three *kos* from the Imperial army, seized a number of bullocks, belonging to the Banjaras, while they were grazing, and were driving them off to their quarters. Mu'azzam Khan and . . . led a detachment of the Imperial forces after them, to inflict chastisement upon them, and release the cattle. Pressing forward with all speed, they overtook the enemy, killed a great many of them, and rescued all the cattle. Such of the enemy as escaped made off with great difficulty, and the royal forces returned. The wretched Afzal, who had advanced very boldly, when he heard of this disaster, was paralyzed, and fled in consternation from Kalyani, without even waiting for the fugitives to come in, and fell back upon his other forces. Mahabat Khan then raveged Kalyani, and continued his march. Every day the black-coated masses of the enemy appeared in the distance, but they continued to retreat. . . .

On the 8th Rajab, Jan Muhammad and Afzal and Rustam, the son of Randaula, and others of the enemy, with about 20,000 horse, made their appearance near the royal army, and were very bold and insolent. . . . Mahabat Khan left his camp in charge of Subhan Singh, and marched out against them. The enemy began to discharge rockets upon the right wing under the command of Diler Khan, and a battle followed. . . . Mahabad Khan was a good soldier; and when reports were brought to him from all parts of the field, he saw that Ikhlas Khan and Diler Khan were hard pressed. . . So he charged the enemy with such impetuosity that they were filled with dismay and fled. The victors followed in close pursuit, and many of the fugitives fell by their swords.

Aurangzeb, having left Mu'azzam Khan and Ikbal Khan in charge of Bidar, on the 23rd Rajab marched against Kalyani. On the 29th he reached that place, and on the same day he reconnoitred the fortress and invested it. . . . On the 8th Sha'ban the approaches were advanced to the edge of the ditch, and the besieged were hard pressed. (*Several actions with and victories over the enemy. The country ravaged. Kulbarga occupied.*) When the ditch was filled with stones and earth, and the bastions and ramparts had been well battered, on the 27th the assailants placed their ladders and mounted a bastion which had been much damaged, and began to undermine and throw down the wall. The besieged made a gallant resistance, and kept up a heavy discharge of rockets, arrows, and muskets. Grenades, naphtha-balls, and trusses of burning straw were thrown from the top of the walls. But the assailants pressed bravely on, and victory was not far off. At this juncture Dilawar Habshi, who with 2,500 men held the place for 'Adil Khan, felt himself in great danger of destruction, and on the 29th wrote a letter begging for forgiveness and offering to surrender. Most of the garrison were Musulmans, so the commandant and all his men were allowed to march out with their property and their wives and families. On the 1st Zi-l ka'da, 1068, the keys of the fortress were given up, and the Prince entered and had the *khutba* read. The commandant sought and obtained permission to go to Bijapur).

ILLNESS OF THE EMPEROR

(Suddenly, on the 1st Zi-l ka'da, 1067 A.H., the Emperor was attacked with serious illness in the form of strangury, constipation and other sympathetic affections, so that he was unable to attend to worldly affairs. Physicians tried all the remedies of their art, but in vain, for the disorder increased. . . . In Safar, 1068, the health of the Emperor had so improved that he was convalescent,. . . and great rejoicings followed).

THIRTY-SECOND YEAR OF THE REIGN

In the eyes of his father the Emperor, Prince Dara Shukoh was superior to his brothers both in merit and age. When his other sons departed to their respective governments, the Emperor, from excessive love and partiality, would not allow Dara Shukoh to go away from him. He also evinced the greatest partiality and affection for the Prince, previding for his honour and dignity. . . .

Shah Buland Ikbal (Dara Shukoh) took upon himself to interfere in the direction of affairs of State, and induced His Majesty to do many unwise things which tended to create disturbances. He urged that Murad Bakhsh had diverged from the path of rectitude, and had not ceased to act improperly. It was therefore advisable to remove him from the *suba* of Ahmadabad, and to settle upon him the *jagir* of Birar. If he obeyed the Emperor's order and proceeded to Birar, his offences might be forgiven and clemency be extended to him. But if, from want of foresight and intelligence, he should prove refractory and disobey the orders, he should be suitably chastised and be brought to Court under restraint. Dara Shukoh then spoke of Prince Aurangzeb. and represented that a party of intriguers had artfully led him astray, and *nolens volens* had persuaded him that he had been worsted by the malice and revenge of his brother (Dara Shukoh), and that he should get the assistance of his brother (Murad Bakhsh), who had resolved upon rebellion.[8] He should then march with the splendid army under his command to the capital, under the pretence of paying a visit to his father, and wherever he passed he should subvert the authority of the Government. To carry out his aims Aurangzeb had set himself to win over to his side great nobles of the State, some of whom he had made his own, and that he was endeavouring to effect his object by secret communications before his designs should become public. The money which he had received as tribute from

[8] *Here the MSS. differ, and the meaning is not certain.*

Kutbu-l Mulk he had spent without permission in the raising of forces, and it would not be long before he would cast off his obedience and commence a war. It was to be hoped that the army which had been sent by the Emperor for the reduction of Bijapur, and was now with Aurangzeb, might not be won over by the money which he had received as tribute; for assuredly, if this were so, it would be a great danger to the State, which it would be almost impossible to avert. The first thing to be done was to send *farmans* recalling all the nobles and their forces from the Dakhin. Then a strenuous effort should be made to get possession of the treasure. By these means the strength and greatness of the Prince would be diminished, and the friends and allies, the strength of his cause, would fall away. . . .

Although the Emperor showed no haste in adopting these views, he was quite willing to send the letters. He could not resist the influence Prince Dara had obtained over him. So letters of the unpleasant purport above described were sent off by the hands of some of the Imperial messengers. The messengers reached Prince Aurangzeb as he was engaged in directing the operations against Bijapur, and he had the place closely invested. The arrival of the messengers disturbed the minds of the soldiers, and greatly incensed the Prince; so, much confusion arose. Some of the nobles, Mahabat Khan, Rao Sattar Sal, and others, went off to Agra without leave or notice. Mu'azzam Khan also, who was the head and director of this campaign, acted in a very ungenerous and foolish way, and wanted to go off to Agra, quite regardless of the duty and respect he owed to the Prince.

This want of support from his followers, and the anxiety he felt about the Emperor, led the Prince to accept the proposals of the people of Bijapur. Having settled this difficult matter, he marched towards Aurangabad; and as soon as he arrived there, he sent messengers in a courteous way[9] to Mu'azzam Khan, desiring him to come and have an interview. The Khan would not listen to the invitation, and acted in a manner unworthy of a great noble. So the Prince ordered Prince Sultan Muhammad to set forth with all speed and use every expedient to bring the Khan to his presence. When the directions were carried out, and the Khan arrived, Aurangzeb immediately provided for his punishment, and sent him prisoner to the fort of Daulatabad. He seized all his treasure, elephants and other property, and gave them into the charge of the State treasurers.)

RAJA JASWANT

(After the defeat of Shah Shuja', and the return of Aurangzeb to Agra, the Emperor sent a force . . to inflict salutary punishment upon Raja Jaswant. The Raja feeling himself unable to resist, in his great perplexity and alarm, sent some of his servants to Dara Shukoh, who, previous to the Raja's flight, had arrived at Ahmadabad, and, without waiting to recover from his toilsome journey through the sandy desert, was busily occupied in gathering forces. . . . Dara Shukoh, having satisfied himself by taking from the promise-breaking Raja a covenant which the Raja confirmed with the most solemn Hindu pledges, marched towards his country. The Emperor was meanwhile moving towards Raja Jaswant's territory, and he wrote the Raja a letter, in which expostulations and threats were mingled with kindness. This letter greatly alarmed the Raja, so that he departed from Dara and returned to his own country. Making use of Mirza Raja Jai Singh, he wrote a penitent and submissive letter to the Emperor, begging forgiveness for his offences; and the Emperor in his clemency forgave him, granted him the *subadari* of

[9] *"Az rah i madara," which many mean either "by way of courtesy" or "by way of dissimulation."*).

Ahmadabad, and sent him a *farman,* bestowing honours and promising favours.)

FATE OF THE PRINCES SULAIMAN SHUKOH, SULTAN MUHAMMAD AND MURAD BAKHSH

(The *zamindar* of Srinagar, having consented to surrender Prince Sulaiman Shukoh, sent him to Court in the custody of his son. Two days after his arrival, the Prince was brought into the Emperor's presence, who directed that on the morrow he, along with Prince Sultan Muhammad, should be sent to the fort of Gwalior, and that both should be fed with *koknar.*[10]. . . .The sons of 'Ali Naki, who had a charge against Murad Bakhsh for the murder of their father, were sent to Gwalior, with directions, that after a lawful judgment had been given, the retaliation for blood should be exacted from the Prince. When they arrived at Gwalior, an inquiry was made by the Kazi. The Prince was resigned to his fate, and said, "If the Emperor will accept my pledges and spare my life, no harm will hapen to his throne; but if he is resolved to take my life, there is no good in listening to such low fellows as these. He has the power, and can do what he likes." On the 21st Rabi'u-s sani, 1072, under the orders of the Kazi, two slaves killed the Prince with two blows of their swords. He was buried in the fort of Gwalior. In the month of Shawwal Prince Sulaiman Shukoh died from the treatment of his jailors, in the thirtieth year of his age, and was buried beside Murad Bakhsh.)

SHAH-JAHAN-NAMAS

[Besides the *Shah-Jahan-names* noticed at length, there are among the MSS. borrowed by Sir H. M. Elliot, several others bearing the same title. 1. "An abstract of the lengthy *Shah-Jahan-nama*" (the *Badshah-nama*) of

[10]*Otherwise called "pusta," a slow poison prepared from poppies.*

'Abdu-l Hamid Lahori. This was written in 1225 A.H. (A.D. 1810), by Muhammad Zahid. 2. A fragment of another and lengthy *Shah-Jahan-nama,* by Mirza Jalalu-d din Tabataba. 3. A short work by Bhagwan Das, which gives brief notices of the ancestors of Shah Jahan, beginning with Adam. 4. A poem by Mirza Muhammad Jan Mashhadi. This is called *Shah-Jahan-nama,* but the title given to it by the author would rather appear to be *Zafar-nama.* 5. Another *Shah-Jahan-nama* in verse, by Mir Mahammad Yahya Kashi.)

SHAH JAHAN-NAMA
OF
MUHAMMAD SADIK KHAN

(The author of this history of Shah Jahan was Muhammad Sadik, who was *Waki'-navis* in attendance upon Prince Shah Jahan in his campaign against the Rana during the life of Jahangir. He afterwards received the title of Sadik Khan. The work embraces the reign of Shah Jahan "from his accession to the throne unto the termination of the confinement into which he fell through the stupidity of Dara Shukoh." A copy of the work in the British Museum ends with the deposition of Shah Jahan, but the author adds that the deposed monarch lived eight years in captivity. Sir H. Elliot's MS. goes on without any break to the end of the reign of Aurangzeb; but to have written all this, Sadik Khan must have lived over a century. The history of the reign of Aurangzeb turns out to be the same as that the *Muntakhabu-l Lubub* of Khafi Khan, with some slight variations. not greater perhaps than Col. Lees found in various MSS. of that work.[11]

The history is of moderate extent, and is written in a simple style. Similarity or indentity in many passages shows that Khafi Khan used the work for his history of the reign of Shah Jahan. There is also among Sir H. M. Elliot's MSS. one called *Tabakat-i Shah-Jahani*, written by the same author. This consists of notices of the great and distinguished men of the reign of Shah Jahan. The names are numerous, but the notices are short.)

[11] *Journal Royal Asiatic Society, N. S. vol. iii. p.* 473.

MAJALISU-S SALATIN
OF
MUHAMMAD SHARIF HANAFI

The *Majalisu-s Salatin,* or "Assemblies of the Sultans" was written by Muhammad Sharif Hanafi. The reason he assigns for writing it is, that 'no one had courage enough in his time to wade through long histories, especially mentioning those of Zia Barni, Kazi 'Ajaz Badshahi, and 'Abdu-l Kadir, which are each works of considerable size, and he therefore determined, notwithstanding his constant avocations, to write an abridged history of India. In the midst of a hundred interruptions, he set himself to the work, but, short as it is, he was nearly failing in his resolution to complete it, and "a wind arose occasionally which was nearly making his pen fly away like an arrow from a bow, and converting his paper into a flying kite." At last he asked his spiritual teachers for their aid and countenance, and through their encouragement he brought it to a completion.

The same irresolution and want of leisure seem to have deprived us of the account of his travels, which, as will be seen from one of the following extracts, extended to a distance quite unusual in his days. He had travelled from Madura in Southern India to Kashmir, and had dwelt for some time in the intermediate countries; and he tells us that if he had recorded all the wonderful things he had seen, he might have filled a thousand volumes. He was employed in some public capacity during the whole time that he was making these tours, for he signifies that he was a person of no mean consideration.

The work was composed in the early part of Shah Jahan's reign, in the year 1038 A.H. (1628 A.D.), according to a chronogram at the close of the work in which the date is recorded.

MUHAMMAD SHARIF HANAFI

The *Majalisu-s Salatin* is not divided into chapters, but the following abstract will show the pages where the principal dynasties and reigns commence and end.

CONTENTS

Size—12 mo. containing 258 pages, each of 9 lines.

The copy from which the following Extracts are taken is in one of the Royal Libraries at Lucknow. I know of no other.

(The Extracts were translated by a *munshi* and corrected by Sir H. M. Elliot).

EXTRACTS

Anecdotes of Muhammad Tughlik

After some time, intelligence was brought that Malik Bahram Abiya, the adopted brother of Sultan Tughlik Shah, had revolted in Multan, and put 'Ali Akhti to death, whom Sultan Muhammad 'Adil had sent with orders to summon the rebel. The Sultan, with a view to subdue the rebellion, marched from Daulatabad towards Dehli, and thence reached Multan by successive marches. Malik Bahram came out to oppose him, but was defeated and slain. His head was brought to the Sultan, who was about to order a general massacre of the inhabitants of Multan, and make streams of blood flow, when the staff of the world, the most religious Shaikhu-l Hakk, came bare-headed to the King's court, and stood before him soliciting pardon for the people. The Sultan forgave them for the sake of that holy man. In short, this King called himself just, and generally before executing persons he certainly did refer the case for the decree of the expounders of the law.

It is said of him, that one day, having put on his shoes, he went on foot to the court of Kazi Kamalu-d din, the Chief Justice, and told him that Shaikh-zada Jam had called him unjust; he demanded that he should be summoned and required to prove the injustice of which he accused him, and that if he could not prove it, he should be punished according to the injunctions of the law. Shaikh-zada Jam, when he arrived, confessed that he had made the assertion. The Sultan inquired his reason, to which he replied, "When a criminal is brought before you, it is entirely at your royal option to punish him, justly or unjustly; but you go further than this, and give his wife and children to the executioners that they may do what they like with them. In what religion is this practice lawful? If this is not injustice, what is it?" The Sultan remained silent; and when he left the court of the Kazi, he ordered the Shaikh-zada to be imprisoned in an iron cage, and on his journey to Daulatabad he took the prisoner with him on the back of an elephant. When he returned to Dehli, on passing before the court of the Kazi, he ordered the Shaikh-zada to be brought out of the cage[1] and cut to pieces. Hence it may be learnt that he possessed very opposite qualities. He was called by the common people "the unjust." There are many similar stories of the actrocities he committed. Tyranny took the place of justice, and infidelity that of Islam. At last he was seized with fever, and departed to the next world, when he was in the vicinity of Thatta, on the 21st Muharram, A.H.

[1] *A few years later we find the Raja of Golkonda imprisoned in an iron cage by Sultan Kuli Kutb Shah.—Brigs' "Firishta," vol. iii. p. 374.*

752 (20th March, 1351 A.D.). The period of his reign was twenty-seven years.

ACCESSION OF SHAH JAHAN

When Nuru-d din Muhammad Jahangir died, the second Lord of the Conjunction, the rightful heir, Shah Khurram, who was entitled Shah Jahan, was in the Dakhin at a distance of three months' journey from the place where the Emperor Jahangir had died. It is well known to politicians that the throne of royalty cannot remain vacant for a moment, and therefore the ministers of the government and the principal officers of the Court considered it expedient to place Sultan Dawar Bakhsh, the grandson of the Emperor Jahangir, upon the throne for some days; and thus to guard against mutinies and disturbances which might otherwise arise. They defeated Shahriyar, who, through his vain ambition, had proclaimed himself King in Lahore. The Emperor Shahabu-d din Muhammad Shah Jahan (may his dominions and reign increase, and may the world be benefited by his bounty and munificence!) also came with a powerful army *via* Gujarat and Ajmir, and soon arrived at Agra. which was the seat of his and his forefathers' government. He mounted the throne of sovereignty in the fort of Agra on Monday the 7th of Jumada-l akhir, corresponding with the 25th of Bahman; and distributed largesses and rewards among his subjects. May the Almighty keep this generous and world-conquering King under His protection and care!

REVENUES OF HINDUSTAN AND THE DAKHIN

It also entered into the mind of this "most humble slave of God" to write a short account of the different provinces of Hindustan, and make it a portion of this small work. detailing how much of this country was in possession of the Emperor Jalalu-d din Muhammad Akbar and his son Nuru-d din Jahangir, and into how many *subas* it is now divided.

MAJALISU-S SALATIN

Be it not concealed that the whole country of Hindustan, which is known to form one-fourth of the inhabited world, and reckoned as the largest of all the countries, is divided into fourteen *subas,* or provinces.

First, the Province of Dehli; revenue upwards of 65,61,00,000 *dams.* Second, the Province of Agra, which is the seat of government; revenue 82,25,00,000 *dams.* Third, the Province of the Panjab, or Lahore; present revenue, 82,50,00,000 *dams.* Fourth, the Province of Kabul, including Kashmir, etc.; revenue 25,00,00,000 *dams.* Fifth, the Province of the Dakhin, or Ahmadnagar; revenue 28,35,00,000 *dams.* Sixth, the Province of Khandesh and Birar; revenue 87,32,00,000 *dams.* Seventh, the Province of Malwa; revenue 28,00,00,000 *dams.* Eighth, the Province of Gujarat; revenue 50,64,00,000 *dams.* Ninth, the Province of Bihar, including Patna and Jaunpur; revenue 31,27,00,000 *dams.* Tenth, the Province of Oudh with its dependencies; revenue 23,22,00,000 *dams.* Eleventh, Province of Ajmir with its dependencies; revenue 42,05,00,000 *dams.* Twelfth, the Province of Allahabad; revenue 30,70,00,000 *dams.* Thirteenth, the Province of Sind, including Multan, Thatta and Bhakkar; revenue 40,00,000 *dams.* Fourteenth, the Province of Bengal, which is equal to two or three kingdoms; revenue 50,00,00,000 *dams.*

The revenue of all the territories under the Emperors of Delhi amounts, according to the Royal registers, to six *arbs* and thirty *krors* of *dams.* One *arb* is equal to a hundred *krors* (a *kror* being ten millions), and a hundred *krors* of *dams* are equivalent to two *krors* and fifty *lacs* of rupees. Each of the fourteen provinces above mentioned formed the territory of a powerful king, and was conquered by the sword of the servants of the Chaghatais. Nine of these fourteen provinces have been visited by the poor compiler of this book, and the following is a detail of them.

THE AUTHOR'S TRAVELS

He was born in the province of the Dakhin, and lived five years there. Though it is mentioned as one province, yet the whole territory of the Dakhin, through which he travelled with his father, consists of five provinces. Ahmadnagar is one province, Bijapur is another, Golkonda is a third; the Karnatik, which is a large territory extending as far as Setband Rameshwar, forms a separate province. Khandesh and Birar, which are in reality two provinces, though rated above only as one, were visited throughout every space of their whole extent by the writer, who has also travelled over the provinces of Gujarat, Malwa, Ajmir, Dehli, and Agra, as well as those of the Punjab or Lahore, and Sind, which includes Thatta, Bhakkar and Multan. By the favour of God, he possessed authority in all these provinces, and visited them as a person of consideration. If he were to note down the wonders and curiosities of all the places he had seen he would require to blacken paper equal to one thousand volumes. He has therefore avoided enlarging his work.

He may, however, as well mention, that when in the territory of the Karnatik, he arrived in company with his father at the city of Southern Mathura (Madura), where, after a few days, the ruler died and went to the lowest hell. This chief had 700 wives, and they all threw themselves at the same time into the fire. This event was related by the compiler of this book at Barhanpur, in the presence of the Nawab Khan-khanan, son of Bairam Khan; but the Nawab did not believe it. The *vakil* of the Raja of the Karnatik, whose name was Kaner Rai, was also present at the court of the Nawab; and when inquiries were made of him respecting the truth of my assertion, he related the event exactly as the writer had done. So the Nawab entered it in his note-book.

All the people of this territory are idolators, and eat all the wild animals of the forest. There is not a single

Musulman there. Occasionally a Musulman may visit the country, deputed by Nizam Shah, 'Adil Shah or Kutb Shah, but the natives are all infidels. The Madari *malangs* and *jogis* go by this road to Sarandip and the hill-fort of Ceylon, which is the place where the impression of Adam's footstep is preserved.

In A.H. 1031 the writer of this book visited the delightful land of Kashmir, when he accompanied the victorious camp of the Emperor who had an army as numerous as the stars. *viz.* Nuru-d din Muhammad Jahangir, and was in the immediate service of the most exalted and noble Nawab, the Great Khan, the best of all the descendants of the chosen prophet, the chief of the house of 'Ali, a nobleman of high rank and dignity. *viz.* Kasim Khan. may God preserve him!

LUBBU-T TAWARIKH-I HIND
OF
RAI BHARA MAL

The author of this brief history was Bindraban, son of Rai Bhara Mal, and was himself also honoured with the title of *Rai*. We learn from the Conclusion of the *Khulasatu-l Insha* that Rai Bhara Mal was the *diwan* of Dara Shukoh: and it is probable, therefore, that our author was early initiated into a knowledge of public affairs. He says that the reason of his entering on this undertaking was that, "after meditating upon the conquests made by the Timurian family in this country, upon their being still more enlarged by 'Alamgir (Aurangzeb) up to the year 1101 A.H., and upon the fact of their continuing uninterruptedly in the possession of the same family, he thought of writing a book which should briefly describe how, and in what duration of time, those conquests were achieved, should give the history of former kings, their origin, and the causes which occasioned their rise or fall, the period of their reign, their abilities and enterprises, and which should more particularly treat of the great conquests made by 'Alamgir."

"It is true," he continues, "that former historians have already written several works regarding the history of ancient kings, and especially Abu-l Kasim, surnamed Firishta, whose compositions are very good as far as regards the language, but the defect of that work is that, notwithstanding its being an abstract, it is in many parts too prolix." Adverting also to the fact that his history does not extend beyond the thousandth year of the Hijra, and hence the important transactions of one hundred years are altogether omitted, he thought it expedient to extract its essence, and compile, with his own additions, a new work, to be called the *Lubbu-t Tawarikh*, or "Marrow of Histories."

He gives as another reason for the superiority of his work over others, that it treats of the extensive and resplendent conquests of the Emperor 'Alamgir, whose kingdom extended towards the East, West, and the South to the seas, and towards the North to the boundaries of Iran and Turan, a vast dominion, to the tenth of which no other kingdom is equal. Perhaps Rum only might enter into competition with it, but even in that case "seeing is better than hearing."

CONTENTS

Preface, pp. 1—3.

Section I.—The Kings of Dehli, from Mu'izzu-d din Muhammad Sam to Aurangzeb, pp. 4-256.

Section II.—The Kings of the Dakhin, viz., the Bahmani, 'Adil-Shahi, Nizam-Shahi, Kutb-Shahi, the 'Imad-Shahi and Baridia, or the Kings of Kulbarga, Bijapur, Ahmadnagar, Golkonda, Birar, and Bidr, pp. 256-329.

Section III.—The Kings of Gujarat, pp. 330-352.

Section IV.—The Kings of Malwa, pp. 352-374.

Section V.—The Kings of Khandesh and Burhanpur, pp. 375-386.

Section VI.—The Kings of Bengal, pp. 386-398.

Section VII.—The Kings of Jaunpur, 399-403.

Section VIII.—The Kings of Sind, pp. 403-408.

Section IX.—The Kings of Multan, pp. 408-410.

Section X.—The Kings of Kashmir, pp. 410-412.

Size.—8vo. pp. 412, of 15 lines each.

Major Scott has made great use of this work in his "History the Dakhin," but so brief a work is of little use. The author quotes no authorities in his preface except Firishta, but he mentions also in the body of the work the *Akbar-nama* and *Jahangir-nama* as being so common as to render it unnecessary for him to enlarge on the periods of which they treat.

The exact year in which the work was composed is somewhat doubtful. It is not quite clear from the pretace whether the date should be rendered 1,100 or 1,101 A.H. A chronogram given by an early transcriber makes it 1106; and if the title of the work be intended to form a chronogram, which is nowhere stated by the author, the date would be 1,108 A.H. (1,696 A.D.).

The *Lubbu-t Tawarikh-i Hind* is very common in India. One of the best copies I have seen is in the possession of Nawab Hasan 'Ali Khan of Jhajjar, written in 1148 A.H. In Europe also it is not uncommon. There is a copy of it in the British Museum (No. 5618). There is also an illegible copy at Paris (Gentil. No. 44) under the incorrect title of *Muntakhabu-t Tarikh.*

(The translations of the following Extracts were revised by Sir H. M. Elliot.)

EXTRACTS

Shah Jahan abolishes the Ceremony of Prostration

It had long been customary with the subjects of this state to prostrate themselves before the King in grateful return for any royal favours conferred on them, and on the receipt of royal mandates. This just King (Shah Jahan), on his accession to the throne. commanded that the practice should be abolished, and, at the representation of Mahabat Khan (Khan-khanan), he established instead the practice of kissing the ground. This also being afterwards found equally objectionable, the King, actuated by his devotion and piety, ordered that it likewise should be discontinued; and that the usual mode of salutation by bowing and touching the head should be restored, with this difference, that, instead of doing so only once, as before. the act should be performed thrice several times. Circular orders, enforcing the observance of this practice, were issued to all the Governors within the royal dominions.

PROSPERITY OF THE COUNTRY DURING SHAH JAHAN'S REIGN

The means employed by the King in these happy times

to protect and nourish his people; to punish all kinds of oppressive evil-doers; his knowledge on all subjects tending to the welfare of his people; his impressing the same necessity upon the revenue functionaries, and the appointment of honest and intelligent officers in every district; his administration of the country, and calling for and examining annual statements of revenue, in order to ascertain what were the resources of the empire; his showing his royal affection to the people, and expressing his displeasure when necessary; his issuing stringent orders to the officers appointed to the charge of the crown and assigned lands, to promote the increase and welfare of the tenants; his admonishing the disobedient, and constantly directing his generous attention towards the improvement of agriculture and the collection of the revenues of the state;—all these contributed in a great measure to advance the prosperity of his empire. The *pargana*, the income of which was three *lacs* of rupees in the reign of Akbar (whose seat is in the highest heaven!), yielded, in this happy reign, a revenue of ten *lacs*! The collections made in some districts, however, fell short of this proportionate increase. The *chakladars* who, by carefully cultivating their lands, aided in increasing the revenue, received marked consideration, and *vice versa.*

Notwithstanding the comparative increase in the expenses of the State during this reign, gratuities for the erection of public edifices and other works in progress, and for the paid military service and establishments, such as those maintained in Balkh, Badakhshan, and Kandahar, amounted, at one disbursement only, to fourteen *krors* of rupees, and the advances made on account of edifices only were two *krors* and fifty *lacs* of rupees. From this single instance of expenditure, an idea may be formed as to what the charges must have been under others. Besides, in times of war, large sums were expended, in addition to fixed salaries and ordinary outlay. In short, the expenditure of former reigns, in comparison with that of the one in question, was not even in the proportion of one to four; and yet this King, in a short space of time, amassed a treasure which it would have taken several years for his predecessors to accumulate!

SHAH JAHAN'S JUSTICE

Notwithstanding the great area of this country, plaints were so few that only one day in the week, viz. Wednesday, was fixed upon for the administration of justice; and it was rarely even then that twenty plaintiffs could be found to prefer suits, the number generally being much less. The writer of this historical sketch on more than one occasion, when honoured with an audience of the King, heard His Majesty chide the *darogha* of the Court that although so many confidential persons had been appointed to invite plaintiffs, and a day of the week was set apart exclusively with the view of dispensing justice, yet even the small number of twenty plaintiffs could but very seldom be brought into Court. The *darogha* replied that if he failed to produce only one plaintiff, he would be worthy of punishment.

In short, it was owing to the great solicitude evinced by the King towards the promotion of the national weal and the general tranquillity, that the people were restrained from committing offences against one another and breaking the public peace. But if offenders were discovered, the local authorities used generally to try them on the spot where the offence had been committed according to law; and in concurrence with the law officers: and if any individual, dissatisfied with the decision passed on his case, appealed to the Governor or *diwan*, or to the *kazi* of the *suba*, the matter was reviewed, and judgment awarded with great care and discrimination, lest it should be mentioned in the presence of the King that justice had not been done. If parties were not satisfied even with these decisions, they appealed to the chief *diwan,* or to the chief *kazi* on matters of law. These officers instituted further inquiries. With all this care, what cases, except those relating to blood and religion, could become subjects of reference to His Majesty?

AN EXTRACT FROM 'ALAMGIR-NAMA OF MD. KAZIM

Illness of Shah Jahan

(On the 8th Zi-l hijja, 1067 A.H. (8th September 1657), the Emperor Shah Jahan was seized with illness at Dehli. His illness lasted for a long time, and every day he grew weaker, so that he was unable to attend to the business of the State. Irregularities of all sorts occurred in the administration, and great disturbances arose in the wide territories of Hindustan. The unworthy and frivolous Dara Shukoh considered himself heir-apparent, and notwithstanding his want of ability for the kingly office, he endeavoured with the scissors of greediness to cut the robes of the Imperial dignity into a shape suited for his unworthy person.[1] With this over-weening ambition constantly in his mind, and in pursuit of his vain design, he never left the seat of government. When the Emperor fell ill and was unable to attend to business, Dara Shukoh took the opportunity of seizing the reins of power, and interfered with everything. He closed the roads against the spread of news, and seized letters addressed to individuals. He forbade the officers of government to write or send any intelligence to the provinces, and upon the mere suspicion of their having done so, he seized and imprisoned them. The royal princes, the great nobles, and all the men who were scattered through the provinces and territories of this great empire, many even of the officials and servants who

[1](*Passages like this frequently occur, but after this they have been turned into plain language in the translation.*)

were employed at the capital, had no expectation that the Emperor would live much longer. So great disorders arose in the affairs of the State. Disaffected and rebellious men raised their heads in mutiny and strife on every side. Turbulent *raiyats* refused to pay their revenue. The seed of rebellion was sown in all directions, and by degrees the evil reached to such a height that in Gujarat Murad Bakhsh took his seat upon the throne, had the *khutba* read and coins struck in his name, and assumed the title of King, Shuja took the same course in Bengal, led an army against Patna, and from thence advanced to Benares.)[2]

The End

[2]*For further details about Shah-Jahan and his reign see "Memoirs of Jahangir" and "Aurangzeb" by Khafi Khan.*